W9-BJF-022

Success Guideposts for African-American Children

Success Guideposts for African-American Children

A guide for parents of children
ages 0–18 years

WILL HORTON

W. Whorton & Company
Chicago

Success Guideposts for African-American Children
by Will Horton

This publication is designed to provide information in regard to the subject matter covered. It is sold with the understanding that the publisher or author is not engaged in rendering legal, accounting, or other professional services. If legal advice or other expert assistance is required, the services of a competent professional person should be sought.

W. Whorton & Company
1900 East 87th Street
Chicago, IL 60617
773-721-7500

Scriptures noted "NIV," taken from the HOLY BIBLE, NEW INTERNATIONAL VERSION. Copyright © 1973, 1978, 1984 by International Bible Society. Used by permission of Zondervan Publishing House. All rights reserved.

The "NIV" and "New International Version" trademarks are registered in the United States Patent and Trademark Office by International Bible Society. Use of either trademark requires permission of the International Bible Society. Scriptures noted "NKJV" taken from the HOLY BIBLE, New King James Version, Copyright © 1982 by Thomas Nelson, Inc.

Manufactured in the United States of America
Library of Congress cataloging in publication data
Horton, Will
Success Guideposts for African-American Children/Will Horton, 1st edition
Includes Appendix and Index
Library of Congress Catalog Card Number: 98-96474
ISBN: 1-892274-15-9 (hbk)
Self-esteem skills for African-American Children 2. Parenting I. Title
Photos by Debra Meeks Photography

DEDICATION

To my mother Eldora Jenkins-Horton. Although she died when I was 14 years old, her early teaching and character development gave me guideposts to live by. Thanks Mom, for your love; wisdom, and commitment to all of us.

This book is also dedicated to my son Will Horton, Jr. and to all African-American children—from children living in poverty to children living in prosperity. It doesn't matter where you are or who you are, it does matter who you think you are and what you expect to become. Dream big dreams; you can succeed. You are only limited by your own imagination and self-expectancy.

You, _____

have the inherent power to be successful in life.

_____

Will Horton

CONTENTS

PREFACE

The idea for writing this book came from a meeting I had with Notre Chatman, director of learning resources at Chicago State University, in which we were discussing the needs of young African-American children and what we could do to help them. The conversations from this meeting were so profound that they began to resonate the needs I had heard—hundred of times from African-American parents—during my 20 years of work as an educator and administrator. As a college professor and president of a successful early childhood development center, I have been asked by a multitude of parents for information on successful parenting techniques and guidelines for success.

The purpose of this book is to provide guideposts for successful African-American parenting. The guideposts were developed from my experience as an educator and as a parent.

Some children who attended my early childhood development center, upon entering first grade, tested one and two grade levels above first-grade levels on standardized achievement tests. These students continue to make the honor roll and succeed in school. Many parents ask me what is the formula for our success? The formula is very simple: As a school we set high achievement standards; we expect and encourage children to learn; we ask parents to form a partnership with the school to work to help their children learn and succeed; and we hire caring and nourishing teachers who expect children to learn.

All children—regardless of social dysfunction, poverty, parental income and education, and exposure and experience to violence—can be successful. African-American children can overcome the serious social, cultural, and economic challenges to their development and to the high level of academic and career failure. The purpose of this book is to help parents help their children become successful by providing guideposts and secrets for success. This book is about helping African-American children to realize their dreams. All children can be successful in life and realize their dreams if they—have *faith* in themselves; have *hope* that the future offers great opportunity for career and personal growth; have a definite *purpose* in life; are *persistent* in reaching their goals; are *determined* and *expect* to succeed; and *work hard* to achieve academic excellence and success in life.

I would like to thank all of our fine teachers who work very hard everyday to help young African-American children develop their minds. A special thanks to all who have contributed to our success: Hope Babb, Lola Barnes, Mary Blackburn, Robert Booker, Anna Brown, Tasha Carothers, Barbara Davis, Edna Dillard, Bertha Gross, Pamela Hodge, Dorothy Horton, Patricia Hoskins, Diana Richardson, Marie Stewart, Marcella Stevenson, Michelle Towns, Tracey White, and Bobbie Wilson.

A special thanks to Mary Jones, my administrative assistant, for typing the manuscript, for her patience during my many revisions, and for her enthusiasm in completing the manuscript. She really made writing this book much easier for me with her generous time and energy; and to my editor, Jane Crouse, for her commitment to excellence and invaluable editorial guidance.

Also, special thanks to all of the parents, volunteers, and supporters of our academic mission: Richmond Burks, Varletta Burks, Chicago City Council Woman Lorraine L. Dixon, Debra Green, Kerry Van Isom, William Jackson, Vera Jelks, Roger Kimbrew, Unece Kimbrew, Dr. Lyman Parks, Mable Raines, Rhonda Richmond, Marcia Smith, Hayes Thompson, and Vanessa Welch. May God continue to bless you and your children.

Finally, a sincere thanks to Donna Beasley for sharing valuable information about the publishing industry. Donna must be commended for her efforts to promote African-Americans in publishing, and to E. Duke McNeil for your legal advice, positive words of encouragement and support.

Success Guideposts for African-American Children

CHAPTER 1

The Significance of Self-Esteem in African-American Children

A student in a third-grade class, in a low-income area on the south side of Chicago—where drugs are sold openly on the streets, where street gangs are fighting for turf and control of the community, and where drive-by shootings, rape, robbery, stabbing, and homicides occur frequently—told her teacher in a class discussion about goals and what students wanted to be when they grow up, that "she would probably be dead."

This statement illustrates the effect violence can have on the hope, faith, and self-esteem of a young mind. According to the teacher, the student's grades and test scores were low. She did not return homework. She had trouble concentrating in class, refused to participate in class discussions, and showed no desire and enthusiasm for learning. For confidentiality reasons, I will use the assumed name, Mary. The tragedy is a precious young child—only eight-years-old—has lost hope and faith in the opportunities life can offer. Because of low self-esteem, Mary feels that she is shackled to the boundaries of her environment and the prism of opportunity appears to be a distant and unreachable dream.

A classmate of Mary, whom I'll call John, has witnessed the drug-related murder of a relative. John has attendance and behavioral problems. He expresses moments of intense anger and becomes easily frustrated. He has frequent temper tantrums, shows no desire for learning, and has low academic skills. Mary and John are typical of children with low self-esteem who have been exposed to violence. Children who do not have hope and faith in society, and see no real future in life, are at great risk of failure, dropping out of school, joining a gang, and becoming juvenile delinquents.

According to the National Center for Education in Maternal and Child Health (Isaacs 1992, v), "living in a context of violence contributes to nihilism, to a sense of impending death and a 'live for today' attitude that limits the futures of these children. It is not surprising that children whose lives are bounded by violence have trouble concentrating in school, see little reason to work hard and experience high failure rates."

Earl T. Braxton, president of Edge Associates, in his NCEMCH presentation, "Violence Within and Without: The Failure of Black Mental Health Systems in Treating Angry Black Children" (1992, 53–54), states that "Angry African-American children suffer from: (a) a sense of disempowerment and lack of control over their lives; (b) a sense of hopelessness/helplessness (dependency); (c) no history around which to build a positive self-image; (d) feeling violated; (e) feeling abandoned; and (f) having lost the boundaries between self and a destructive or disorganized environment."

The need for a positive self-concept and self-esteem building skills for African-American children is didactically illustrated in the NCEMCH publication *The Impact of Community Violence on African-American Children and Families*. "More and more young African-American children and family members witness or are exposed to violent behavior in their daily lives. A recently completed study of fifth graders in a school located in an economically deprived area of New Orleans found that 40 percent of these 10-year-olds had seen a dead body, 72 percent had witnessed weapons being used, and 49 percent had observed a wounding" (Isaacs 1992, 10). A similar 1990 study conducted by John Richters in a school in Washington, D.C., located in an area considered to be only moderately violent, found that 12 percent of the fifth and sixth graders had been shot, stabbed, or sexually assaulted, and 22 percent had witnessed someone else being shot, stabbed, or sexually assaulted (Isaacs 1992, 53–54).

Similar findings and statistics have been gathered for children in other inner-city areas. A survey of 1035 children, ages 10 to 19 years, in several Chicago public schools, found that 75 percent of the participating boys and 10 percent of the participating girls had directly witnessed the shooting, stabbing, robbing, or killing of another person (Isaacs 1992, 10).

Researchers have found that the glorification of violence has led many African-American youth to have a casual attitude toward violence. The value of life has also been diminished, because many African-American males do not expect to live to 25 or 30 years of age. With little hope and faith in the future, going to jail, killing, and dying are no big deal.

Recent research from the U.S. Department of Justice (1996, 1) suggests that "exposure to violence during childhood and adolescence may lead to substance abuse, delinquency, [and] adult criminality and contributes to emotional problems." Because of this high exposure to violence, it becomes necessary for all adults to explore ways to ameliorate African-American children's resilience to overcome life's social ills caused by early exposure to violence. Hope Hill, a professor in the department of psychology at Howard University, in a presentation to the NCEMCH (Isaacs 1992, 25–29), found that

> A great many children experience chronic violence on a daily basis and are still able to triumph over these enormous stressors and grow to be healthy social and emotional individuals. Possible protective mechanisms which the researchers have

observed and seen in the lives of children exposed to community violence include the following: (1) early bonded primary relationships which promote social development; (2) an adult who can buffer community violence; (3) experiences which promote affective development; (4) promotion of cultural awareness and positive cultural identity; and (5) an explicit value system that eschews violence.

These protective mechanisms Hill suggests can be programmed into preventive interventions with children exposed to violence in the following ways.

- Promoting the understanding of culture and fostering a positive sense of cultural identity. Culture may well serve as a protective mechanism by strengthening identity development, providing an ethos, creating a sense of belonging, and expanding a child's world view.
- Developing a specific value system that guides self-development, social relationships, conduct, and a sense of self-worth.
- Providing opportunities for children and families to receive debriefing and supportive treatment after situations of community violence so that they can begin to work through frightening feelings rather that simply repressing the experience.
- Building on spiritual values. This helps children to connect with a higher being and develop a sense of their place in the universe.

African-American children are at risk of emotional maladjustment and failure if parents do not take the responsibility for their children's development. Parents are their children's first and most influential teacher. Parents need to develop a developmental agenda to help ensure, and participate in, the success of their children. Over 30 years of research documents that family involvement has a powerful influence on children's achievement in school. When families participate in their children's education, children can achieve so much more than children whose families are less involved. These achievements include the following:

- Earn higher grades and receive higher test scores.
- Attend school more regularly.
- Have a more positive attitude about and complete more homework.
- Are less likely to drop out of school.
- Are more likely to enroll in and complete higher education.
- Manifest a greater positive self-concept and positive behavior.

There is an urgent need for African-American males to become more responsible fathers and to participate in the child rearing and development of their children. Research from the Office of Juvenile Justice and Delinquency Prevention (1997, 1), states that "children who have an ongoing, positive relationship to their fathers do better in school and get along better with their peers than children without such a relationship. Those children whose fathers play a positive role in their lives also tend to stay out of the juvenile justice system."

African-American families need to adopt and teach their children a paradigm of morals and character ethos. Morals and character are discussed in detail in chapter 8.

WHAT IS SELF-ESTEEM?

Webster's New World Dictionary defines self-esteem as belief in oneself—self-confidence and self-respect. Self-esteem is the total sum of all of an individual's experiences—socially, emotionally, physically, intellectually, and morally. From these experiences a self-identity emerges. Self-identity or self-concept is the perception a person has of him- or herself. Self-identify involves the concept of recognizing oneself, to know oneself. Emphasis is placed on the "I" or "me." The child begins to ask questions such as: Who am I? What do I believe? Can I do things on my own? Am I happy? Am I sad? Am I attractive? Do my friends like me? Am I loved? Am I a good person? Am I good in sports? In the later stages of development the child asks: What can I do best? and What is my purpose in life?

Children are not born with a high or low self-esteem. Each child is born with a brain that includes a blank page—akin to a television or computer screen. This brain has billions of neurons waiting to be routed, connected, and hard-wired—similar to a computer chip. Self-esteem is a learned concept that is shaped by a child's environment and self perception.

To better understand the psychology of self-esteem, an individual has to understand the relationship between the psyche and soma—the mental and physical connection between the mind and body. The mind is made up of all a child's thoughts, feelings, emotions, and memories, both conscious and unconscious. The mind works as a neurotransmitter—akin to a computer chip—processing information through the central nervous system, consisting of billions of cells called neurons or nerve cells. These nerve cells are routed through channels that relay information to the body. The body responds to the sensations of the mind. For example, when the mental state expresses happiness, the body reacts with a smile; when the mental state expresses sadness, the body reacts with a sullen look; and when the mental state express anger, the body reacts with a frown. The mind and the body are interconnected. The mind (mental state) + body (physical state) = the child or ego. If the mind believes something the body will express it. If children think they are dumb, they will act dumb and do dumb things. In other words, children will act out these thoughts of the mind, known as a self-fulfilling prophecy. Children will become what they believe and expect to become. If children have no hope and faith in the future, they will become desensitized and devalue life. Children will develop a negative, self-destructive behavior when they have a low self-concept. Benjamin Carson, chief neurosurgeon at Johns Hopkins University, stated in a television interview, "I thought, when growing up as a child, that I was dumb, so I did dumb things, like fighting and acting up in class." In addition to being an accomplished physician, today Carson is also a world-famous author.

Children with low self-esteem are at risk of encountering major problems and disturbances. A child with low self-esteem exhibits the following negative characteristics.

- Has a negative attitude about life.
- Experiences anger frequently.
- Is uncooperative.
- Exhibits disruptive behavior.
- Is easily influenced by peers.
- Looks for negatives.
- Makes excuses.
- Blames others.
- Has a poor self-image.
- Shows aggressive behavior.
- Is unable to depend on others.
- Is unable to trust others.
- Is unable to love others.
- Is unable to express love.
- Has low grades in school.
- Becomes easily frustrated.
- Loses temper frequently.
- Drops out of school.
- Joins a gang.
- Becomes a juvenile delinquent.
- Becomes pregnant.
- Abuses alcohol and/or drugs.
- Has eating disorders.
- Commits a crime.

Research has shown that children with high self-esteem are more likely to be successful in school. High self-esteem has been found to enhance children's reading and comprehension skills.

Children with high self-esteem appear to be happy, enjoy learning, and learn easily. A child with high self-esteem exhibits the following positive characteristics.

- Has a positive self-concept.
- Has self-confidence.
- Has self-control.
- Is self-sufficient.
- Has self-respect.
- Has a strong self-identity.
- Has self-discipline.
- Is self-assured.
- Has self-awareness.
- Has a positive self-image.
- Appears to be happy.
- Finds learning fun.
- Self-improves.
- Finds learning less of a challenge and more as an adventure.
- Is responsible.
- Is independent.
- Is cooperative.
- Enjoys a challenge.
- Is enthusiastic.
- Can manage failure.
- Asks for help when needed.

THE SOURCES OF LOW SELF-ESTEEM

Self-esteem is the cumulative evaluation of one's social environment, cognitive development, and perception of self. Self-esteem is also called *self-concept, self-image,* or *self-worth.* As a child grows and develops there are many factors that contribute to low self-esteem. Your child may fail to make the basketball, gymnastics, hockey, baseball, or football team or may not excel in the sport that he has chosen. She may not make the honor roll one semester or make a B or C in a subject area that she felt she should have received an A. He may have received unfair criticism for an attempted project or assignment. She may have experienced a failure or had an experience with or exposure to violence, child abuse, or neglect. African-American children are at greater risk for either becoming victims of violence or being the perpetrators of violence. Young African-American males ages 12–24 years experience violent crime at a rate significantly higher than the rates for other racial groups. Recent research suggests that when children are exposed to violence during early childhood and adolescence, it may lead to future adult criminality including substance abuse and emotional problems. When children experience or are exposed to violence they often suffer from a wide spectrum of child development problems, including the following:

- A low self-concept
- An inability to modulate states of emotions
- A loss of faith and hope in life
- A loss of faith and belief in a fair and just society
- Any sensitivity for morality
- Learning difficulties

The National Institute of Justice study *Evaluation of Violence Prevention Programs in Middle Schools* (1995, 1) found that "adolescents are at high risk for violent crime. Although they make up only 14 percent of the population age 12 and over, 30 percent of all violent crimes—1.9 million were committed against them." Students in four selected urban middle schools had a great deal of experience with and exposure to violence. At the start of the study, 40 percent of the students stated that they had seen someone shot or stabbed, and 20 percent said that their own lives had been threatened. Critical evidence suggests some of the early adolescence problems of African-American children, such as learning disabilities, dropping out of school, drug and alcohol abuse, teenage pregnancy and early parenthood, delinquency, and violence are interconnected, and antisocial, promiscuous, sexual, and substance abuse behaviors are mutually related. Child abuse and neglect are also factors that lower self-esteem. The number of child abuse and neglect cases is increasing each year. In 1997, over three million children were reported for child abuse and neglect to child protective service agencies in the United States, according to the National Committee to Prevent Child Abuse. The estimated number of children in foster care is more than one-half million and increasing each year.

Millions of African-American children are at risk of failure because of poverty and its effects on young children and families. Poverty is one of the root causes of a low self-esteem. Poverty increases the likelihood of children suffering from a wide spectrum of social, emotional, physical, and educational problems. Many of the problems African-American children encounter living in poverty can have a negative cumulative effect throughout their lives. Many African-American children are able to overcome the cancer of poverty because of positive parental, family, school, spiritual, and community relationships, and the resilient and innate desire by some to succeed.

Scientific research has documented the venomous influence poverty has on the development, health, self-concept, and future of African-American children. In 1996, 58.2 percent of African-American children under 18 years of age who lived with a female head of household, with no spouse present, lived in poverty. Children living in poverty are at developmental risk, and are likely to die in infancy because of poor or absent prenatal care, and/or due to a lower-than-average birth weight. Low-birth-weight babies have a higher health risk of developing learning disabilities and emotional and neurodevelopmental problems. Children living in poverty likely do not receive adequate nutrition. Nutrition affects children's ability to learn. Children living in poverty are at risk of being prenatally exposed to alcohol and/or other illicit drugs. Children living in poverty are likely to experience or be exposed to violence, and to have developmental delays, which will affect their school readiness and ability to learn.

The problems caused by prenatal substance abuse have devastating effects on African-American children and their families and create serious educational challenges for the children. The National Institute on Drug Abuse (NIDA) found that "A mother who uses drugs risks her life and her baby's [life]." According to NIDA, some of the health risks attributed to illicit drug use are

- Prematurity
- Low birth weight
- Infection
- Small head size
- Sudden infant death syndrome
- Birth defects
- Stunted growth
- HIV/AIDS
- Learning disabilities
- Neurological problems

Further research findings from the NIDA (1998, 1) found that "Children with histories of prenatal polydrug exposure, which included cocaine, scored significantly lower on standardized test measures of language development (Receptive and Expressive Subtests of the Sequenced Inventory of Communicative Development—Revised) than nonexposed children."

The NIDA conducted a survey in 1992–1993 to determine the depth of illicit drug use among pregnant women. The survey reported that 221,000 women used illegal drugs during their pregnancy. Illegal drug use was higher for African-American women—7500 in relation to their percentage of the population (NIDA 1992, 1).

All of the developmental risk factors discussed can have a negative impact on children if these factors are not addressed by parents, teachers, and other individuals involved in the child's development. As parents pay greater attention to the factors influencing their children's lives, parents will be in a better position to help their children overcome the environmental toxins and barriers to responsible citizenship and success in life.

Because of the sensitivity and delicate nature of self-esteem, even a child with high self-esteem can have events in his or her life that will lower self-esteem. The individuals in the child's learning environment also contribute to his or her low self-esteem. These individuals include parents, relatives, role models, and teachers who do not promote positive self-esteem.

Parents are their children's first and most influential teacher. It is important that parents become role models for their children and manifest the positive self-esteem and self-concept they want their children to emulate. Thus, all parents need to evaluate their self-concept and their knowledge of positive self-esteem skill-building techniques. The following sections will help you take a close look at your parenting style, self-esteem concept and techniques, decision-making style, and self-perceptions.

Purpose of Self-Esteem Evaluation

The purpose of the self-esteem evaluation is to empower parents to become more successful by teaching positive concepts, evaluating parenting styles and techniques, making a self-discovery, and changing any self-defeating approaches to successful parenting.

This questionnaire will challenge you to think critically about your parenting style, and strengthen your understanding and significance of the effect self-esteem can have on your children's development and academic performance.

Instructions

For each statement, put a check mark in the appropriate column that best describes your answer. Do not rush. Take as much time as you need. Answer each question honestly. Your answers should reflect your genuine belief. Review the answers. Make any corrections if necessary.

Self-Esteem Evaluation for Parents			
	Strongly agree	Agree	Disagree
1. A strong self-concept enhances self-esteem.			
2. Negative words can lower self-esteem			
3. Positive words can help increase self-esteem.			
4. It is important to use positive praises with children.			
5. A negative word and a negative action send a negative message to children.			
6. A positive word and a positive action send a positive message to children.			
7. Self-esteem helps to bring about self-fulfillment.			
8. What you think is self-validating—if you think you will fail, you will fail.			
9. If you think you will become a winner, you will become a winner.			
10. Self-esteem helps a child to become aware of his or her true potential.			
11. A child with high self-esteem is more likely to be more disciplined.			
12. A child with high self-esteem is more likely to cope with delayed gratification.			
13. A child with low self-esteem is more likely to have lower grades in school.			

continued

Self-Esteem Evaluation for Parents			
	Strongly agree	Agree	Disagree
14. A child with low self-esteem is more likely to join a gang.			
15. If children expect to succeed they will succeed.			
16. Children should be taught that mistakes and failures are learning opportunities.			
17. Spanking children is not the most effective way of gaining discipline.			
18. Children learn best when parents model expected behavior.			
19. Children learn to become independent when they are given responsibility.			
20. What parents do is more important than what parents say.			

Answer Key

If you answered all questions strongly agree, you have an excellent knowledge and understanding of self-esteem. If you answered agree to any of the questions, you have a good knowledge and understanding of self-esteem. If you answered disagree to any of the questions, you need improvement in self-esteem building skills.

One of the ways to teach effective self-esteem building skills is to "practice what you teach." Parents often expect their children to "do as we say, not do as we do." Parental actions and messages can be confusing to children. Parents need to model the behavior they expect from their children.

I would like to share with you a handout that I give parents at my lectures, counseling sessions, and early childhood development center.

The Role of the Parent

P   **is for powerful.**
Parents are their children's first teacher and have the most influence in shaping and molding the self-concept of their children. The power to develop successful children lies within the parents. Carl Jung puts the power and influence factors in their proper perspective: "Nothing has a stronger influence psychologically on their environment, and especially on their children, than the unlived lives of the parents."

A   **is for ability.**
Every child is born with a brain and nervous system of approximately 10 billion to 100 billion nerve cells, waiting to be shaped and routed to the mind. It is the parents' responsibility to foster the care, nourishment, growth, and development of their child's mind. Children are born with the following abilities or senses: sight, hearing, taste, smell, and touch. The mind is a blank page waiting to be shaped by loving parents. A child's ability and growth development process reminds me of a statement by Epictetus: "Nothing great is created suddenly, any more than a bunch of grapes or a fig. If you tell me that you desire a fig, I answer you that there must be time. Let it first blossom, then bear fruit, then ripen."

R   **is for responsibility.**
Teach your children responsibility. Children who develop a responsible character develop one of the most important building blocks for success in life. This is what President John F. Kennedy had to say about responsibility: "Our privileges can be no greater than our obligations. The protection of our rights can endure no longer than the performance of our responsibilities."

E   **is for education.**

All children, regardless of race or socioeconomic background, should have access to state-of-the art, high-quality educational programs, which include preschools, elementary and high schools, trade and business schools, and colleges and universities. Specific national educational goals should be established for all school levels, beginning with preschool, to meet the educational needs of all children in America in the new millennium. Malcolm X stated so eloquently that "Education is our passport to the future, for tomorrow belongs to the people who prepare for it today."

N   **is for nourishment.**

Some of the most important factors that contribute to the success of a healthy self-esteem and growth development of children is not food for the body, but food for the brain. Parents should express love, show affection, communicate, play, and spend quality developmental time with their children. The following foods for the brain will build self-esteem and self-concept skills that will last a lifetime.

- Express love and show affection by touching and hugging. Neuroscientists have found that physical affection promotes brain growth.
- Spend quality developmental time by reading to your children and having your children read to you. Reading to your children helps them to learn word sounds and sentence structure.
- Talking to your children helps build reading and vocabulary skills.
- Playing with children has been found to increase their ability to learn.
- Sing to your child. Music is a learning tool that can teach new skills and make learning more fun. Let your child sing to you; this enhances self-esteem.

Parents should not take the responsibility of nourishing young children lightly. Children are the world's future. Grayson Kirk taught us, "Our greatest obligation to our children is to prepare them to understand and to deal effectively with the world in which they will live and not with the world we have known or the world we would prefer to have."

T **is for teach.**

Webster's New World Dictionary defines teach as "to show or help a person to learn how to do something; guide the studies of; give lessons; help someone develop; provide a person with knowledge and give instruction." Do you want to release your responsibility as your children's most influential teacher to a stranger? I am sure your answer was no. Do you want to guide and enhance your children's learning? Do you want to play a part in your children's development? Is it the parents' responsibility to provide knowledge and instruction to children? I am sure your answers were yes to all of these questions. In the future you should look at yourself as a person with dual responsibilities—parent and teacher. Become a partner in your children's learning and development. Plan and participate in your children's educational pursuits. Take the lead in ensuring that your children's social, emotional, intellectual, physical, and cognitive skills are developed. Teach your children basic values and self-esteem building skills. Help your child develop a passion for learning. The Proverb (22:6), states it best: "Train up a child in the way he should go, and when he is old, he will not depart from it." (NKJV)

References

Braxton, Earl T. 1992. Violence within and without: The failure of black mental health systems in treating angry black children. In *Violence: The impact of community violence on African-American children and families,* edited by Mareasa R. Isaacs. Arlington, Va.: National Center for Education in Maternal and Child Health.

Hill, Hope. 1992. How community violence affects critical aspects of development of urban African-American youth. In *Violence: The impact of community violence on African-American children and families,* edited by Mareasa R. Isaacs. Arlington, Va.: National Center for Education in Maternal and Child Health.

Isaacs, Mareasa R., Ph.D. 1992. *Violence: The impact of community violence on African-American children and families.* Arlington, Va.: National Center for Education in Maternal and Child Health.

National Institute on Drug Abuse. 1992. *Pregnancy and drug use trends.* Rockville, Md.: National Institute on Drug Abuse.

National Institute on Drug Abuse, National Institute on Drug Abuse, Infant, Child, and Adolescent Workgroup. 1998. *Consequences of prenatal drug exposure—Research findings.* Rockville, Md.: National Institute on Drug Abuse.

National Institute of Justice. August 1995. *Evaluation of violence prevention programs in middle schools.* Washington, D.C.: U.S. Department of Justice, Office of Justice Programs, and National Institute of Justice.

Office of Juvenile Justice and Delinquency Prevention. 1997. *Responsible fatherhood.* Washington, D.C.: U.S. Department of Justice, Office of Juvenile Justice and Delinquency Programs.

U.S. Department of Justice. November 1996. *Assessing the exposure of urban youth violence.* Washington, D.C.: U.S. Department of Justice, Office of Justice Programs, and National Institute of Justice.

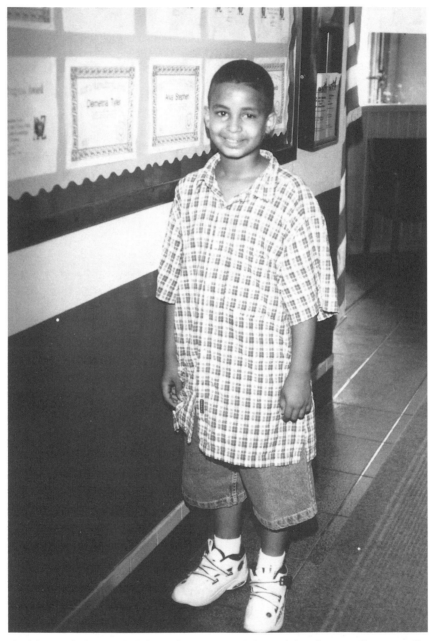

Self-confident children have confidence in themselves and their abilities. They believe that they have the power and abilities to complete tasks successfully.

CHAPTER 2

The Sources of Self-Esteem

Self-esteem is made up of two components: confidence in oneself and confidence in one's abilities. Self-confident children are determined, positive, self-assured, and self-reliant. They are composed, well-balanced, proud, and believe in their ability to deal with life challenges. Children with self-confidence make appropriate decisions, feel good about their accomplishments, and manifest pride in themselves. They feel that the ability to control life's challenges is within themselves.

Children are not born with self-esteem but learn self-esteem. Words are powerful and can build or lower self-esteem. Low self-esteem proliferates as a result of inconsistent and negative messages and images received from parents, caregivers, and the environment. According to Deborah Rees, a licensed dietician, "If a child tends to be overweight or obese typically children make fun of [him or her]. This leads to low self-esteem. It may also lead to underachievement in the classroom because teachers don't expect as much from the child."

Steven Shelo and Robert E. Hannemann, in *Caring for Your School-age Child: Ages 5 to 12* (1995, 125), suggest that "Self-esteem is the way a person thinks and feels about himself and how well he does things that are important to him. Self-esteem is shaped by what a child thinks and expects of himself, and by how important people in his life think about him. His self-esteem is high when the way he sees himself comes close to his 'ideal self'—how he would like to be."

Characteristics of Self-Confident Children

Self-confident children have confidence in themselves and their abilities. They believe that they have the power and abilities to complete tasks successfully. Self-confident children are self-assured, poised, self-reliant, self-sufficient, secure, assertive, and positive, and have established a definite and firm belief system. The self-confident child with a positive self-concept makes the following statements.

- I have the ability to handle problems.
- I have people that I can depend on.
- I can do things on my own.
- I have people who love me.
- I make good decisions.
- I can do many things.
- I will not quit.
- I am a winner.
- I am special.
- I can do it.
- I like me.

Characteristics of Children with Self-Respect

Self-respect is the proper respect for oneself and one's worth as a person. Having self-respect includes being proud of oneself, being self-sufficient, and having high self-esteem. A child with self-respect exhibits pride; has high self-esteem, and is self-reliant, self-confident, self-respecting, and independent. A child with self-respect makes the following statements.

- I am happy that I can help myself.
- I am proud of my decisions.
- I deserve good friends.
- I am proud of myself.
- I deserve to be loved.
- I can do many things.

- I am a winner.
- I love myself.
- I am special.
- I am smart.

DEVELOPING SELF-CONFIDENT, SELF-RESPECTING CHILDREN

By using positive praises and actions, parents can help their children build a positive self-concept, develop a belief in themselves, and guide their pursuit of finding the ideal self. Words can wound a child's self-concept and can contribute to a negative belief system. For example, using sexist words can limit young girls' perception of self, career, and aspirations, and can lower self-esteem. Factors such as stereotyping, prejudice, and discrimination may contribute to children's low self-esteem.

Sexist Language

Practice using nonsexist words. For instance, words ending in "man" promote the idea that the occupation can only be held by men. The mosaic of American gender roles has changed. In the past, the American culture portrayed a "male human resource development theme," in which careers were focused on the man. Female advocates and scholars found this emphasis to be sexist and promoted equal rights for women. Below are some examples of the effective use of nonsexist words.

Inappropriate	Appropriate
Policemen serve and protect the public.	Police officers serve and protect the public.
The mailman delivers the mail.	The mail carrier delivers the mail.
The fireman put out the fires.	The firefighters put out the fires.
The motorman operates the train.	The engineer operates the train.

continued

Inappropriate	Appropriate
The salesman sells merchandise.	The salesperson sells merchandise.
The newsman reports the news.	The newsperson reports the news.
The gas man reads the meters.	The meter reader reads the meters.
The patrolman directs the traffic.	The patrol person directs the traffic.

Racist Language

Use nonracist words and terminology. Using racist words can help contribute to low self-esteem.

Acceptable term	Preferred term
Blacks	African-Americans
Indians	Native Americans
Orientals	Asian-Americans
Mexicans, Puerto Ricans	Hispanics

Diminutive Names

Avoid using diminutive names. Diminutives names and words can contribute to low self-esteem. Examples include the following:

- How did you get into those pants, Fatty?
- You are the ugly duckling in the family.
- Move over so cross-eyed Jane can see.
- We cannot use anyone your size, Tiny.
- What do you want, Skinny-Minnie?
- Play with the babies, Small Fry.
- Cry Baby, what is wrong now?
- Head is wearing a cap today.
- Wear your cap Bald Head.
- You are so bull headed.
- Brush your buck teeth.
- Close your big mouth.

- Here comes Little Bit.
- Stand up Pot Belly.
- Hello, Midget.
- Hi, Bow Legs.

Nicknames

Avoid using nicknames. Nicknames describe a child's appearance, personality, and self-image. Negative nicknames can damage a child's self-esteem.

Nickname	Negative image
Midget	I am too small.
Monkey man	I am ugly.
Little Bud	I will never grow up.
Blackie	I do not like my skin color.
Baby Do	I am some kind of sideshow.
Long legs	I am too tall and skinny.
Pig	I am too fat.
Little girl	I am not a little girl anymore.
Little Bro	I am growing up and I am not everybody's brother.

FACTORS THAT CAN LOWER SELF-ESTEEM

In addition to language, there are many circumstances that can contribute to low self-esteem in children. As discussed earlier, children are not born with self-esteem, but learn self-esteem. A low self-esteem is not contagious, as many childhood diseases are. In order to change the self-esteem of a child, parents, teachers, and others must change the child's perception of self. If a child has low self-esteem, the factors that may have contributed to it must be analyzed.

There are four primary sources that influence self-esteem development: the child's environment, home, school, and socioeconomic status. The source of low self-esteem is most likely to come from one or all of these primary sources. The home is the place that has the most influence on children's self-esteem and positive self-development. Parents are their children's first and most influential teacher, and the home should serve as a safety net for children, protecting them from the toxins of the environment and other negative sources. The home environment should provide love, safety, and security from the negative elements children may encounter. Parental influence will be discussed in more detail in chapter 9.

The home is where the building blocks of self-esteem should begin. As parents, you may not be able to change your children's environment and socioeconomic status but you can help change your children's attitude by helping them develop a positive self-concept and plant the seeds that will help them develop a positive attitude.

If the message and action are negative, the result will be low self-esteem. The formula for a low self-esteem is: Negative words and actions + Negative message = Low self-esteem.

Negative words and negative actions create a powerful message that you are sending to your children. Remember, words can wound a child's self-concept. What type of messages are you sending to your children? When used frequently, negative words and negative messages can be very damaging. Negative words and actions develop pessimistic children—those with low self-esteem who become hopeless and expect the worst from life. The following negative words, actions, and messages can contribute to a child's low self-esteem.

Negative words and actions	Negative messages
You are dumb.	I do not have the ability to learn.
You should have gotten more As on your report card.	No matter how hard I try, I am always criticized. I am a failure.

continued

Negative words and actions	Negative messages
I do not have the time to visit your school.	I am not important. Everybody's mother and dad took the time to visit the school except mine. I feel very sad when I see my friends' parents at school. I feel alone.
Your grades are the lowest in your class. Everybody is smarter than you.	I need help with my homework. I am too dumb to understand what I am to do. I will just forget about my homework and watch TV.
You always forget everything.	I do not have any brains. I cannot think like other people.
You are a failure. I cannot do anything with you.	I cannot improve my behavior. I am no good. I wish I could run away and no one could find me.
I have to punish you all the time because you are bad.	I am always doing something wrong. I am a bad person. Nobody loves me.
Stop crying like a baby.	I cannot express my emotions and feelings without being put down.
I am sorry that you are my child.	I am unwanted and helpless.
You will never grow up.	I am immature and will not amount to anything in life.
You do not know how to follow directions.	I cannot learn to do things.
You are not worth two cents.	I am not worth anything. I am of no value to anybody, not even to myself.
You are the worst child I have.	I am different. I do not belong to this family. I am treated differently. I have to act out to be noticed.
Another C. I did not expect you to do any better. You are a slow learner.	I will get a D the next time. It really won't make any difference. Nobody has any high expectations of me anyway.

continued

Negative words and actions	Negative messages
I have lost all my patience with you.	There is no hope for me. No one is kind to me or willing to help me to become a better person. It is all my fault.
I give up on you. You are too bad for me to do anything with you.	I do not have anybody to care for me. What am I going to do? It is my fault that nobody loves me.
You always make mistakes. You cannot do anything right.	I am the only one who makes mistakes. I am a failure.
You are a failure at everything you try.	There is no need for me to try to do anything. I am already a failure. What is the use? I cannot achieve anyway.
I do not like you because you remind me of your father who left us.	I did not do anything. I cannot help who I look like. I am innocent. Why am I the scapegoat?
Get out of my face now. I'm tired of looking at you.	I am unloved by others. I cannot love myself if my parents do not love me.
No, I will not hug you.	Nobody loves me. I hate myself.
Ask your teacher to read you a story. I do not like to read unless I have to.	How will I ever learn to read and enjoy listening to stories if I do not see anybody in my family reading? The teacher cannot give me all of her time. Maybe I will just give up on listening and learning to read.
You may not play because you are being punished.	Everybody else is playing and having fun while I am being punished. I am always punished for everything no matter what. I am the worst thing in the world.
I am not going to buy you a book. You cannot read anyway.	I am dumb. I will never learn to read. Nobody is willing to help me learn to read.

continued

Negative words and actions	Negative messages
I am ignoring you.	I cannot get any attention no matter how I try. Whatever I do good or bad nobody pays me any attention. I am nobody.
I do not want to hear it. It does not make sense whatever you are trying to say.	No one wants to listen to what I have to say. My needs and thoughts are not important.
You are not going to the movie with us because you did not clean your room.	Nobody loves me. If I had cleaned my room I would have been punished for something else. I am always left out of everything.
You may not go on the field trip with your class.	I feel left out. I am not allowed to be with my classmates and have fun on the trip.
You are going to take piano lessons. All of your friends are playing the piano already.	I have to do what others are doing. I do not want to learn to play the piano. My feelings about what I want to do are unimportant. Why do I have to be punished for something I do not like?
Put your paper in the waste basket. All of your answers are wrong.	I cannot do anything right.
Play by yourself. My mother did not play with me when I was growing up.	I am not good enough for you to take a little time to play with me. I have to entertain myself all the time. I have no one to interact with through play.
Do not talk to me I am busy. I do not have time to talk to you.	Nobody has the time to listen to me. What I have to say is not important. I am a misfit in this family.
I cannot say that I love you.	Nobody ever tells me they love me. I am not going to love anybody. Maybe I am not loveable.

continued

Negative words and actions	Negative messages
Cry as long as you wish. I am not going to do anything. You will get tired of crying and stop eventually.	Nobody cares about my feelings and emotions. I need someone to touch me and tell me I am special. I am all alone.
Shut up before I hit you in your mouth.	I am so bad. I cannot open my mouth. I am no good.
I refuse to let you eat your dinner tonight because you have been bad at school.	I am being punished unfairly. I am hungry. Everyone else is eating. Why should I have to miss my dinner? My sister does bad things. She never has to miss her meals. Nobody loves me.
I must lock you in your room because you spilled your milk—again.	Everybody spills something sometimes. I am the worst person in the world. I should tear up everything in this closet. I am no good anyway.
If you stop crying I will give you a piece of candy.	She is trying to bribe me. I will take the candy. I will go along with it. I will cry again when I want some more candy. She is too soft. I will be the winner.

SELF-ESTEEM SELF-EVALUATION: NEGATIVE WORDS

The purpose of this evaluation is to help you become aware of the power negative words can have on your children's self-esteem. Negative words are powerful and can wound self-esteem.

What negative words have you used with your children?	What is the negative message?	What are you going to do to change your use of negative words?
1.		
2.		

continued

What negative words have you used with your children?	What is the negative message?	What are you going to do to change your use of negative words?
3.		
4.		
5.		
6.		
7.		
8.		
9.		
10.		

SELF-ESTEEM SELF-EVALUATION: NEGATIVE ACTIONS

The purpose of this evaluation is to help you become aware of the power negative actions can have on your children's self-esteem. Negative actions are powerful and can wound self-esteem.

What negative action have you exhibited with your children?	What is the negative message?	What are you going to do to change your pattern of negative actions?
1.		
2.		
3.		
4.		
5.		
6		
7.		

continued

What negative action have you exhibited with your children?	What is the negative message?	What are you going to do to change your pattern of negative actions?
8.		
9.		
10.		

Reference

Shelo, Steven, and Robert E. Hannemann. 1995. *Caring for your school-age child: Ages 5 to 12.* New York: Bantam Doubleday Dell.

Use positive praises and actions with your children. The objective of using positive praises and actions is to highlight the accomplishments and efforts of the child, to give the child hope, courage, and confidence; and to help foster a positive self-concept and character development.

CHAPTER 3

How to Use Positive Praises
and Actions Effectively

Using positive praises and actions, also called Positive Mind Concepts™, can contribute to a child's positive self-concept. Positive praises and actions focus on the desired behavior instead of the child's deficiencies or failures. Positive praises encourage and reward responsible behavior rather than criticizing or punishing the child for failure or misconduct. What parents say—words, and what parents do—actions, build their children's maturity and self-confidence. These psychoconcepts™ can be effective tools to help children build self-esteem. African-American children need to build a strong positive self-concept to serve as a buffer against the negative forces of society, such as violence, racism, poverty, peer influence, exposure to drugs, failure, competition, and other life-challenging factors.

Praise means to express approval or admiration. The objective of using positive praises and actions is to highlight the accomplishments and efforts of the child; to give the child hope, courage, and confidence; and to help foster a positive self-concept and character development.

There is a debate in academic circles between the use of praise versus encouragement. Some experts think that if parents praise children they will become dependent on their parents' approval and later become dependent on others' approval. I disagree with this, and feel that positive praise can be used successful—if parents praise the children's efforts and accomplishments—not just the children. By praising their children's efforts, parents show that they are interested in their children and care about them and what they do. Effective praise also expresses appreciation and approval and transmits to children the expected behavior.

Remember, children living in a home where negative words and actions are used by their parents have low spirits, are melancholy, have a sense of futility, and can lose their purpose in life. They become hopeless and have no zeal for learning. Negative words and actions cause children to become pessimistic, whereas children living in a home where positive praises and actions are used by their parents are optimistic and have hope and faith in the future. They are inspired, enthusiastic about life, and have a zeal for learning.

USING POSITIVE PRAISES AND ACTIONS EFFECTIVELY

Here are some techniques to help parents learn to use positive praises and actions effectively.

Praise Children's Positive Behavior

Give praise, recognition, and reward for significant accomplishments, progress, tasks, or efforts successfully completed.

Use Only Positive Words and Actions in Your Parenting Style

Accentuate the positive things your children do, not the negatives. Treat failures as temporary not as final. I like Henry Ford's view on failure: "Failure is only the opportunity to begin again more intelligently." The mistakes and failures young children make are only learning opportunities. Just like a baby learning to walk, he or she may fail at first but will keep trying until walking is a success. This effort reminds me of John Johnson, founder of

Ebony and *Jet* magazines and one of the most successful African-American businesses in the United States. In his book *Succeeding Against the Odds* Johnson states, "Failure is a word that I don't accept." If you have been critical of your children's actions and behavior in the past, stop it now. This may take some practice but you can overcome your urge to criticize by using this technique: Count to 10 before you criticize. Practice becoming a positive parent. If you think positive, you will become positive. Always remember this self-validating statement: You are who you think you are. This goes for parents too.

Communicate with Your Children

Since parents are their children's first and most influential teacher, communication is one of the most important components in your children's development. Research has found that the quality and quantity of communication children receive in their early years directly relates to high levels of self-esteem. Send clear and precise messages to your children. Avoid long and confusing messages, leaving no room for error or miscommunication. Your messages should match the age, development, and attention span of your child. You will set the agenda and sow the seeds for communicating the building blocks of self-esteem.

I like the idea by Kuan Chung, which I revised to more directly relate the point about children and the building blocks of self-esteem. That is, if you plan for a year, plant a seed. If for 10 years, plant a tree. If for a hundred years, teach the children. When you sow a seed once, you will reap a single harvest. When you teach the children, you will reap a hundred harvests.

By teaching positive concepts and sowing the seeds of positive self-esteem you will reap in your children a hundred harvests. When parents communicate effectively with their children, the adults immediately begin to build self-esteem in their children by building self-confidence. If children have self-confidence, they are not afraid to make mistakes. The children's self-image is enhanced because they feel good about themselves.

Recognize the Uniqueness of Your Child

Accept your children as people with specific individual differences. Do not stereotype children. Each child is special and has his or her own qualities, imperfections, and limitations. Do not compare the abilities of one child with another's.

Respect the Rights of Your Children

Madeleine Y. Gomez, clinical psychologist and assistant clinical professor at Northwestern University, has a bright poster that she created which lists the rights of a child. These include that children have the right to be protected against all forms of abuse. Gomez values the individual differences and rights of children. She and her daughter Michelle Gomez have formed a two-person army to promote the rights of children. The poster has been distributed in 20 states. Dr. Gomez says, "It has been great that people have noticed and feel positive about the Rights of A Child poster; with the promotion of kids rights you can change the world." If you would like a free copy of the poster you may write Dr. Madeleine Gomez, P.O. Box 5312, Evanston, IL 60204-5312.

When I first saw the poster I immediately investigated its source and later called Dr. Gomez to purchase the poster. She said that she would be happy to send any number of posters I needed to my early childhood development center without charge because she wanted to promote the rights of children. The Gomezes understands what James Agee with Walker Evans meant when they said, "In every child who is born, under no matter what circumstances, and of no matter what parents, the potentially of the human race is born again."

Children are special; they are our future. As caregivers and parents we have to respect the individual differences and rights of children. I would like to share with you Dr. Gomez's rights of a child.

The Rights of a Child
- The right to special care, if disabled.
- The right to adequate nutrition and medical care.

- The right to learn to be a useful member of society and to develop individual abilities.
- The right to be brought up in a spirit of peace.
- The right to a name and nationality.
- The right to affection, love, and understanding.
- The right to be among the first to receive relief in times of disaster.
- The right to protection against all forms of neglect, cruelty, and exploitation.
- The right to free education and to full opportunity for play and recreation.
- The right to enjoy these rights, regardless of race, color, sex, religion, national or social origin.

Do Not Take Children's Feelings, Emotions, and Ideas for Granted

Use positive words and praises to show your children that you love them. Loving parents have been found to play a significant role in developing and enhancing self-esteem. Schedule a special time of the day or week, preferably daily, to share activities with your children that are important to them. Set a schedule and continue it if possible. Be a role model for your children by setting a positive example for them to follow. Do not set the poor example, "Do as I say, but not as I do." If you live what you teach, your children will respect you and follow your lead. I give the following handout to all parents who enroll their children in my early childhood development center.

**Goals to Protect, Maintain, and Enhance
Children's Self-Esteem**

- Express optimistic confidence in the child's learning potential.
- Strive to kindle a strong desire and inner drive to learn.
- Involve the child in setting goals.
- Treat difficulties and setbacks as a natural part of learning.

---

continued

Goals to Protect, Maintain, and Enhance Children's Self-Esteem

- Provide encouragement, support, and optimism in the face of difficulties.
- Treat failure as temporary, not terminal. "Failure is not final; failure is success not yet received."
- Recognize, praise, and reward learning progress and specific achievements.
- Provide assistance to overcome problems. Redirect the child if necessary.
- Be objective rather than judgmental.
- Compare developmental progress to the child's own level, not to the level of others.
- Focus discipline on negative behavior, not the child as a person. Explain the reason for the discipline and expected behavior.

Will Horton © 1997

Positive Praises and Actions

Positive Mind Concepts (PMC)™, utilized in positive praises and actions, help build self-esteem. PMC develop optimistic children—those with high self-esteem who have hope and faith in the future and expect to succeed. Practice using Positive Mind Concepts™ with your children.

Positive praises	Positive messages
I knew you could do your homework.	I am a responsible person.
You are growing and learning more every day.	I feel good about myself.
Thank you for helping me with the grocery bags. You are getting so strong.	I am growing up. I can help with the chores. I am developing self-awareness and a sense of responsibility.
Your progress reports are great. You are on your way to success.	I can do a good job. I have self-confidence.

continued

Positive praises	Positive messages
You are a winner. You have a very good report card.	I worked hard. I can excel in my class. I feel good about myself.
You completed your homework. I knew you could do it. Great job!	I can do it! I am smart.
You have respect for others.	I can treat others kindly and respectfully.
I like the way you handled the disagreement with your friend.	I am confident. I can handle problems.
I like your painting. What an imagination you have!	I am creative. I can use my own ideas.
You mean a lot to me.	I am special to you. I feel special about myself.
You did an outstanding job of cleaning your room today.	I accept my responsibility. I am proud of myself.
You are special to this family.	I am a part of the family. I am welcome. I fit into the family circle.
You are unique.	I am special. There is no one else exactly like me. I am beautiful.
How nice. You were so kind to your brother.	I am learning to think of others. I am unselfish. I feel good about myself.
You are a good listener.	I can listen. I can follow directions and do what is asked of me.
You did a very good job of cleaning up after yourself in the living room.	I feel proud of myself. I am responsible for cleaning up after myself and putting things back in place.
Thank you for waiting while I talked on the telephone.	I am respectful of others. I am learning to be patient. I have good manners. I feel good about myself.
You know how to treat your friends.	I respect my friends. I love my friends. My self-esteem is enhanced.

continued

Positive praises	Positive messages
You made my day.	I can make you happy. You are pleased with what I did. I feel good about myself.
You have a very good idea.	I have something useful to offer.
Please set the table for dinner. Thank you.	I can share the family chores. I am part of the family.
Let's play a game together.	I am special. Someone is taking the time to play with me.
You may participate in the talent show at school. Your teacher wanted my permission. I know you will be great.	You believe in me. I am going to do my best acting. I have self-confidence. I am going to make you real proud of me.
Here, you try it. Go ahead and make your own lunch.	I can choose. I am responsible. I am growing up. I feel good about myself.
I love you!	I am special. I am appreciated. I love my family and friends. I love myself.
Let's go to the library every week. We'll get you a library card so that you may borrow things.	The library is an important place for learning. It is a resource for all kinds of books and learning aids. I like the library. It has a lot of neat things I can borrow. I am responsible. I must also remember to be quiet at the library.
Could you please help me wash the dishes?	I am a responsible member of this household.
I am going to read your favorite story to you.	I will listen carefully and read along with you. I am happy that you are spending time with me.
Let's watch your favorite TV program and talk about what is happening in it.	My parents care about me and what I see on TV. They want to spend time with me doing my favorite things.
You may help choose the color of paint to decorate the living room.	I can share in family decisions. My family values my ideas.
Please sort the clean socks in the laundry basket.	I can share in household chores. I can learn to match socks according to colors, sizes, and numbers.

continued

Positive praises	Positive messages
You may help me with grocery shopping today.	I am given responsibility. I am trusted. My decisions will be respected. I feel good about myself.
Please put all the pieces back in the puzzle before you put it away.	I can solve problems. I can match shapes. I am responsible for putting things back in place.
Keep on trying to learn to zip your jacket. You are already making a good start.	I can do it. I can learn to zip my jacket.
You may play in the yard until dinner is ready.	I can be trusted. I will go inside when I am supposed to.
You may play after you do your homework.	My homework is important. I must do my homework before I get tired. I am responsible for doing my homework.
Tell me why you are so angry.	My family is concerned about my feelings and emotions. I can talk to my parents about how I feel.
I have a special hug for you today.	I am special. My parent loves me.

SELF-ESTEEM SELF-EVALUATION: POSITIVE PRAISES

The purpose of this evaluation is to help you become aware of the power positive praises can have on your children's self-esteem. Positive praises are powerful and can build self-esteem.

What positive praises have you used with your children?	What is the positive message?
1.	
2.	
3.	

continued

What positive praises have you used with your children?	What is the positive message?
4.	
5.	
6.	
7.	
8.	
9.	
10.	

SELF-ESTEEM SELF-EVALUATION: POSITIVE ACTIONS

The purpose of this evaluation is to help you become aware of the power positive actions can have on your children's self-esteem. Positive actions are powerful and can build self-esteem.

What positive actions have you exhibited to your children?	What is the positive message?
1.	
2.	
3.	
4.	

continued

5.	
6.	
7.	
8.	
9.	
10.	

When children trust and feel loved by their parents and others they develop self-esteem. Parents should let their children know that they love them and accept them as unique individuals.

CHAPTER 4

Guideposts for Building and Enhancing Self-Esteem in African-American Children

Many African-American children are at risk of developing low self-esteem because many of them are exposed daily to factors that lower self-esteem. These factors include violence, racism, poverty, stereotypes, and discrimination. Low self-esteem is one of the main reasons African-American children drop out of school, perform poorly on academic achievement measures, and fail in life. Another impediment to success is cultural neglect by African-American parents. African-American parents must take the responsibility of teaching their children ethnic pride, which will enhance their children's self-concept by better understanding their culture and by being proud of their heritage.

As parents, caregivers, and people concerned within the community about the future of African-American children, we all need to work to enhance their self-esteem. Children's self-esteem is shaped by the evaluations of self and by important adults in their lives. Parents, or the children's primary caregivers, such as foster parents or grandparents, have the most influence on the development of self-esteem. Parents, spiritual institutions, schools, family, friends, and community all have some responsibility to help African-American children develop high self-esteem. The following are some guideposts for developing and enhancing positive self-esteem in African-American children.

Love

Children's self-esteem develops through love. Love is a foundational building block for self-esteem. Through love children develop attachment and trust with the caregivers responsible for them. When children develop trust and feel loved by their parents and others, they develop self-esteem. Parents should let their children know that they love them and accept them as unique individuals. Spend time each day doing activities together such as reading, shopping, or playing games.

Safety and Security

Safety and security build trust, confidence, and self-esteem in children. They feel that someone is there who cares for them and will protect them.

Health

A healthy child is a happy child—one with positive self-esteem. Children with health problems, such as low weight babies, have a higher risk of developing learning disabilities, hyperactivity, emotional problems, and mental illness, according to research from the U.S. Department of Education.

Nutrition

Nutrition affects children's ability to learn and their self-esteem. A child who is hungry may feel that he or she is being punished for doing something wrong or may feel unloved, which leads to a low self-esteem. Research has found that good nutrition helps a child's brain to develop. Make sure your children have balanced and nutritious meals each day.

Sense of Belonging

A positive self-concept is built when children feel good about themselves; when they have a positive image of who they are; and when they have close relationships and connections to others who love them. Allow children to help with various chores in the home. This will help develop responsibility, independence, and a sense of belonging. Self-esteem is also enhanced.

Respect

Respect your children through words and actions. Talk to your children in a respectful and pleasant voice. Remember, children have rights too. Show concern for them, and value their point of view. Express pros and cons of different viewpoints and opinions. Let your children know that you value their thoughts.

Listening

Listening to children lets them know that you are concerned about and value their ideas. Listening to children helps to build self-esteem. By listening carefully and respectfully, parents can model good listening skills expected of their children. These skills include paying attention, listening patiently, avoiding interruptions, and acknowledging nonverbal messages. Children with good listening skills learn better.

Expectations

Expect your children to learn. Set realistic expectations and goals for your children and help them reach their goals through love, support, and guidance. Provide goals that are reachable and allow opportunity for success at different levels.

Responsibility

Responsibility teaches children desirable values. When children learn to become responsible they are not only gaining self-esteem, but they are also learning desirable values such as accountability and independence. Responsibility is one of the most important life skills children should learn. I like what Richard Nixon had to say in an interview with Garnett D. Horner of the *Washington Star News* following Nixon's election to his second presidential term. Nixon said, "The average American is just like the child in the family. You give him some responsibility and he is going to amount to something. He is going to do something. If, on the other hand, you make him completely dependent and pamper him and cater to him too much, you are going to make him soft, spoiled and eventually a weak individual."

Positive Discipline

Positive discipline teaches children to learn self-control and rules of conduct and expected behavior through positive ways. The use of positive discipline helps build children's self-esteem by encouraging desired behavior instead of using the self-defeating approach to discipline such as criticizing, blaming, shaming, or using physical punishment.

What are the benefits of using positive discipline?

- Increases children's self-esteem.
- Teaches children respect, which allows them to feel valued.
- Teaches children to become responsible for their behavior instead of blaming and shaming others.
- Helps children to learn to solve problems. They gain independence.
- Encourages an enthusiasm for cooperation.

For parents who want to learn more about how to develop positive discipline in their children, I suggest reading *Positive Discipline* by Jane Nelson, Ed.D.

Culture

When children are taught ethnic and cultural pride their self-esteem is higher. Teaching African-American culture should be a priority in every African-American family. Culture is a learned concept. Children learn culture through observation and experience. Culture shapes children's values and beliefs. Children's learned cultural values help develop their behavior. If your family culture values hard work and high expectations, and if family members are expected to succeed in life, then your children will be expected to meet your family's cultural standard. Help your children develop a proud ethnic concept and cultural pride. Strong ethnic and cultural pride helps to build self-esteem and resilience in children.

Positive Self-Identity

A positive self-identity will help African-American children prepare for life's challenges. Positive Mind Concepts (PMC)™ have been used to develop positive self-esteem in children by using positive praise and action techniques (see chapter 3). The PMC™ discussed thus far have focused on extrinsic influences such as parents and other individuals who share a close relationship with the child. The objective of positive praise and action is to plant the seeds of positive self-esteem to encourage the permanent self-sustaining, positive self-identity in African-American children.

Intrinsic PMC™ are inner-directed beliefs guided by the internal "I" concept and images children have of themselves. An example is, "I can be successful." PMC™ transmute the external "you" concept self-esteem building skills emphasized in positive praise and action. For example, the statement "you are special" can be transmuted to the positive "I" concept statement "I am special." The "you" concepts used in positive praise and action—if used over a long period—can cause children to become dependent upon others for their self-esteem. For intrinsic PMC™, emphasis is placed on developing internal self-esteem building skills without outside encouragement. Thus, it is inner-directed, such as "I am special."

Intrinsic PMC™ help children develop a high self-identity, which will help them to overcome any identity crisis that may occur while growing up. PMC™ also give children the resilience to buffer any exposure to violence, crime, poverty, prejudice, racism, and discrimination. Intrinsic PMC™ help children to learn to have the following characteristics.

- Self-assurance—confidence in oneself—self-confidence
- Self-confidence—belief in oneself and one's abilities
- Self-control—ability to control one's emotions, desires, and actions without outside influence
- Self-discipline—ability to control one's desires and actions
- Self-image—perception of self; self-identity
- Self-identity—awareness of one's individual identity
- Self-concept—thoughts of the mind; image of self; belief system
- Self-esteem—belief in oneself; pride in self
- Self-respect—respect for self; understanding one's value
- Self-awareness—confidence in self and one's talents and abilities
- Self-discovery—learning one's true abilities and potential
- Self-fulfillment—satisfaction of one's aspirations and dreams
- Self-love—ability to love oneself
- Self-sufficiency—independence; skills necessary to complete a job without outside help
- Self-sustainability—ability to continue a task once it has been started
- Self-efficiency—belief in one's ability to complete a task successfully
- Self-realization—fulfillment of one's potential and abilities in life
- Self-determination—ability to make decisions according to one's own mind or will, without outside influence
- Self-actualization—full development of one's abilities and ambition

Through PMC™ children are able to learn self-sustaining and self-determining, self-esteem building skills by transmitting the "I" thoughts into their subconscious mind. They do this subliminally by affirming the thoughts daily. The brain connects these thoughts to the pathways of the mind much like a computer chip that stores information. When information is stored into the computer's memory, the data can be recalled or accessed at a later date. These psychoconcepts™ process works with the affirmation of the "I" thoughts. Frequent use of PMC™ and the "I" words below help shape the inner child—a child's mind, soul, and spiritual self. When children need the power of a positive self-identity to overcome negatives and other life challenges, they can access these positive beliefs in the mind and will have the resilience to overcome the challenges. Parents should encourage children to affirm these PMC™ daily. Pick one concept each day and have children repeat it for a minimum of 20 times. Children should be in a quiet area, with eyes closed. The children's voices should descend from a high pitch for the first 10 affirmations to a low pitch and whisper near the end. For example,

I am special
I am special
I am special
I am special
I am special
I am special
I am special

I am special
I am special
I am special
I am special
I am special
I am special
I am special
I am special
I am special
I am special
I am special
I am special
I am special

Positive Mind Concepts™	Self-esteem skills established
I am special.	Self-confidence
I am loved.	Self-image
I make good decisions.	Self-confidence and responsibility
I am smart.	Self-esteem and intellectual development
I am unique.	Self-image
I am proud of myself.	Self-love
I make good grades in school.	Self-fulfillment
I am completing my homework on time.	Self-improvement
I can do many things.	Self-efficiency

continued

Positive Mind Concepts™	Self-esteem skills established
I am growing.	Self-realization
I am succeeding in school.	Self-actualization
I am a winner.	Self-image
I am capable.	Self-improvement
I have the ability to succeed in life.	Self-confidence
I am learning to be more responsible.	Self-control
I am learning to be more independent.	Self-assurance
I am a good listener.	Self-control
I like myself.	Self-image
I am important to my family.	Self-identity
I respect others.	Self-control
I am creative.	Self-confidence

PARENTS' EVALUATION OF THEIR CHILDREN'S SELF-IDENTITY

The objective of this evaluation is to help you determine if your children have excellent, good, or low self-identity. Children need a positive self-identity to help them overcome any identity crisis later in life, especially during adolescence. If your children have low self-identity, you and your family will have to work hard to improve it. If your children have an excellent or high self-identity, as a parent, you need to continue to encourage it. Complete the checklist below for each of your children.

	Yes	No
1. Your child feels that he or she is special.		
2. Your child like to do things on his or her own.		
3. Your child has a positive attitude about life.		
4. Your child feels he or she can succeed in school.		

continued

	Yes	No
5. Your child is proud of his or her heritage.		
6. Your child shows pride in self.		
7. Your child feels that he or she is loved.		
8. Your child feels that he or she is part of the family.		
9. Your child feels that his or her views are valued.		
10. Your child shows respect for self and others.		

Answer Key

If you checked yes to all of the questions, your child has an excellent self-identity. If you checked one no answer, your child has a good self-identity. If you checked two or more no answers, your child has a low self-identity. You can improve your child's self-identity by using Positive Mind Concepts™.

It is important for parents to realize that their children's self-esteem is conceived by what the children think and feel about themselves, and by what those in their environment think and feel about the children. Parents should shield their children from negative environments and negative thinking people.

CHAPTER 5

When Should Training in Self-Esteem Begin?

Forces that shape children's self-esteem begin at an early age. At birth, a child is born with a brain and nervous system of approximately 10 billion to 100 billion nerve cells, called neurons. Research by neuroscientists has found that the brain's development process begins before birth, with billions of neurons waiting to be connected to the pathways in the mind. The young brain is influenced by a child's environment, nourishment, stimulation, and overall care. A newborn baby's senses are as follows:

- Sight: A newborn's vision is approximately 10 to 30 times lower than adults' but improves as the baby gets older.
- Hearing: Newborns can hear very well. Research has found that the fetus in the mother's womb may be receptive to sounds and can hear.
- Taste: Studies have found that an infant's ability to taste may be developed before birth.
- Smell: Infants can identify different odors by using facial expressions.

59

- Touch: Infants are sensitive to touch and are able to express pain and pleasure. Infants will tell their parents when they are sad by crying and when they are happy by smiling.

Self-esteem development should begin as early as the last months of pregnancy and continued through adolescence. As noted, research has found that unborn babies can hear sounds during the last months of pregnancy. Expectant parents should talk to their baby. They should tell their unborn child how happy they are about the upcoming birth. Expectant parents should express love and tell their baby how special he or she is to them. During the first months of life, babies begin to develop self-esteem. They have a perception of their environment and attempt to control it. Infants learn to trust parents and caregivers to meet their wants and needs. The positive responses help develop self-esteem and self-worth. As children move through the stages of development, infancy through early childhood, their self-concept will continue to change and evolve. It is important for parents to realize that their children's self-esteem is conceived by what the children think and feel about themselves, and by what those in their environment think and feel about the children. Parents should shield their children from negative environments and negative-thinking people.

At each developmental stage children have unique life challenges. To better understand your children's behavior and their need to have positive self-esteem, it is necessary for you to understand the various stages of child development.

Infant Stage (0–12 months)

Infancy is the child development stage from birth to about 12 months of age. Research has shown that cognitive development in infants is more advanced than most parents realize. Why the need to begin teaching self-esteem at such an early age? Research has documented that infants have memory as soon as they are born. When infants are six months old, they begin to retain long-term memories. One of the primary responsibilities of parents as their children's first and most influential teacher is to help their children succeed and achieve their fullest potential. African-American children face many challenges, including the following:

- Nearly 10 million African-American families live in poverty.
- Over 50 percent of African-American children living with a single parent live in poverty.
- African-American children are more likely than white children to drop out of school.
- African-American children are more likely than white children to live in poverty.
- African-American children are more likely than white children to attend high-poverty schools.
- African-American children are suspended from school at much higher rates than white children. African-American males are suspended at higher rates than African-American females.
- African-American children are exposed to and experience violent crime at significantly higher rates than white children.

The Children's Defense Fund's Moments in America for Black Children (1998) illustrates the challenges African-American children face while growing up. (CDF calculations are based on 180 school days, each of which are 7 hours.) According to the Children's Defense Fund,

- Every 4 seconds a baby is born to a black woman under age 20.
- Every 6 seconds of the school day a black child is suspended.
- Every 29 seconds of the school day a black high school graduate decides not to go to college.

- Every 45 seconds of the school day a black child drops out.
- Every 2 minutes a black baby is born into poverty.
- Every 6 minutes a black baby is born at low birth weight.
- Every 8 minutes a black youth is arrested for a violent crime.
- Every 9 minutes a baby is born to a black woman who had late or no prenatal care.
- Every 48 minutes a black baby is born.
- Every 3 hours a black young adult, age 20–24, is murdered.
- Every 4 hours a black teen is killed by a firearm.
- Every day a black child under 5 is murdered.
- Every day a black child or teenager dies from HIV infection.
- Every 3 days a black infant dies during childbirth.

Parents need to plant the seeds of a positive self-concept while their child's brain is developing and free of any negative concepts—before their child is exposed to those negative concepts from sources such as peer groups, friends, relatives, the media, and other outside influences. The planting and nourishing of these positive mind concepts will develop the child's self-concept, which will improve behavior, attitude, and grades in school, and which will help the child become a successful and productive member of society.

Toddlers (Ages 12–24 months)

The toddler stage is approximately 12–24 months of age. One of the significant developmental changes in the toddler is language development. The child begins to learn words and their meaning.

Some child development researchers have proclaimed that adults should modify their speech—baby talk—to toddlers to make it easier for the toddlers to learn their language. I recommend to parents who come to me for counseling that they use a limited amount of baby talk, only to get their child's attention, but to talk to the child in simple but complete sentences to facilitate word sounds, sentence structure, and vocabulary development.

Early Childhood/Preschool (2–5 years)

Early childhood, sometimes called the preschool years, is the child developmental stage beginning at the end of infancy and extending to 5 or 6 years of age. The statement is often made in early childhood that "the early years are the learning years." During early childhood, preschoolers' cognitive and social development is more advanced than at other stages in life. During this stage, young children learn to explore, discover, and master the environment; become increasingly self-sufficient; and develop relationships with peers. The cognitive and social advances of the early childhood stage play significant roles in developing the child's self-concept. The early years are not only learning years, but windows of opportunity for parents to develop and enhance their children's self-esteem. Every African-American child should not only know that he is unique and beautiful, but she also needs to know the history and contributions African-Americans have made to society.

Middle Childhood (6–12 years)

Middle childhood is the developmental stage from the end of the sixth year to 12 years of age. The need for a strongly developed self-concept and high self-esteem is of immense importance at this stage of development. During this stage, children not only learn the basic and fundamental skills of education but are exposed to greater social interaction; they learn from other children. Cultural and ethnic development also takes place.

Adolescence (12–19 years)

Adolescence is the child developmental stage from approximately 12 years of age to the late teens. The need for a positive self-concept and high self-esteem is even more paramount at this stage. During adolescence greater emphasis is placed on self and identity. The period of adolescence has been called many names including "the terrible teens" and "the turbulent years."

It is necessary for parents to plant the seeds of positive mind concepts™ at an early age—at each stage of development in order to instill in their children a positive identity. In adolescence when children are attempting to establish their own identity and self, parents should be there to encourage and support their children.

In order to help nurture the social, emotional, physical, cognitive, intellectual, and spiritual development of children, parents must gain a greater understanding of the specific needs of children at each developmental stage. This newly acquired knowledge will enable parents to practice successful parenting skills and help their children develop a positive self-concept. At each developmental stage, while some needs will remain the same—such as the need for love and the need for parents to participate in their children's learning—new needs will be added because the child is growing. Each developmental stage presents specific needs for that period.

THE NEEDS OF CHILDREN:
FIVE STAGES OF DEVELOPMENT

Figure 5.1 illustrates the various needs of children throughout their developmental years.

Need	Infant stage	Toddler stage	Early childhood	Middle childhood	Adolescence
1. The need to feel safe and secure	√	√	√	√	√
2. The need for a safe environment	√	√	√	√	√
3. The need to be touched and hugged	√	√	√	√	√
4. The need to be loved	√	√	√	√	√
5. The need to develop trust and faith	√	√	√	√	√

continued

Need	Infant stage	Toddler stage	Early childhood	Middle childhood	Adolescence
6. The need for good nutrition and health practices	√	√	√	√	√
7. The need for patience and quality time	√	√	√	√	√
8. The need for praise and self-esteem building	√	√	√	√	√
9. The need for brain stimulation	√	√	√	√	√
10. The need for communications	√	√	√	√	√
11. The need for guidance	√	√	√	√	√
12. The need for cognitive development	√	√	√	√	√
13. The need to be encouraged	√	√	√	√	√
14. The need for strong family relationships	√	√	√	√	√
15. The need for positive adult role models in the home	√	√	√	√	√
16. The need for parents to participate in their children's learning	√	√	√	√	√
17. The need for consistency and continuity	√	√	√	√	√
18. The need for creative play		√	√	√	
19. The need to discover	√	√	√	√	√
20. The need to achieve			√	√	√
21. The need to develop spiritual values			√	√	√
22. The need to become more self-sufficient			√	√	√

continued

Need	Infant stage	Toddler stage	Early childhood	Middle childhood	Adolescence
23. The need to develop a positive self-concept		√	√	√	√
24. The need to explore		√	√	√	√
25. The need to be more creative		√	√	√	√
26. The need to make new friends			√	√	√
27. The need for greater responsibility			√	√	√
28. The need for age-appropriate learning materials	√	√	√	√	√
29. The need for you to read to me and help me develop an appreciation for reading	√	√	√	√	
30. The need for you to read to me	√	√	√	√	
31. The need for an appropriate reward and discipline policy		√	√	√	√
32. The need for moral development		√	√	√	√
33. The need to express oneself			√	√	√
34. The need to develop a strong self-concept			√	√	√
35. The need to develop ethnic pride			√	√	√
36. The need to learn about one's culture			√	√	√
37. The need to understand self and others			√	√	√

continued

Need	Infant stage	Toddler stage	Early childhood	Middle childhood	Adolescence
38. The need to understand the meaning of gender			√	√	√
39. The need to explore the world and its connection to self			√	√	√
40. The need to develop a self-identity (What about me?)		√	√	√	√
41. The need for a greater understanding of self (Who am I?)			√	√	√
42. The need to be more independent (I can do it.)			√	√	√
43. The need for more responsibility (I can do lots of things.)			√	√	√
44. The need to develop a strong bond with peer group				√	√
45. The need to express love			√	√	√
46. The need for the promotion of reading as a lifelong adventure	√	√	√	√	√
47. The need to know where I am going in life				√	√
48. The need for you to be there for me—I am growing and I need you	√	√	√	√	√
49. The need for attention	√	√	√	√	√

continued

Need	Infant stage	Toddler stage	Early childhood	Middle childhood	Adolescence
50. The need for language development	√	√	√	√	√
51. The need for parents to set learning goals for children			√	√	√
52. The need for acceptance	√	√	√	√	√
53. The need to think critically				√	√
54. The need for parents to understand behavior patterns at each stage of development	√	√	√	√	√
55. The need for respect	√	√	√	√	√
56. The need for self-confidence	√	√	√	√	√
57. The need for a positive self-image		√	√	√	√
58. The need to become more self-reliant			√	√	√
59. The need to become more self-determined			√	√	√
60. The need to develop compassion			√	√	√
61. The need for greater coping skills			√	√	√
62. The need to set goals			√	√	√
63. The need to please parents and others			√	√	√
64. The need to become a successful and productive member of society					√

continued

Need	Infant stage	Toddler stage	Early childhood	Middle childhood	Adolescence
65. The need to be listened to	√	√	√	√	√
66. The need to belong		√	√	√	√
67. The need for positive expectations			√	√	√
68. The need to encourage independence			√	√	√
69. The need for a value system to live by			√	√	√
70. The need for greater patience and sympathy	√	√	√	√	√
71. The need to manage failure		√	√	√	√
72. The need to be happy	√	√	√	√	√
73. The need for resilience			√	√	√
74. The need to make decisions			√	√	√
75. The need to feel special	√	√	√	√	√
76. The need for understanding	√	√	√	√	√
77. The need for protection	√	√	√	√	√
78. The need to accept responsibility			√	√	√
79. The need to learn good manners		√	√	√	√
80. The need to learn family values		√	√	√	√
81. The need to have empathy and sympathy for others			√	√	√

continued

Need	Infant stage	Toddler stage	Early childhood	Middle childhood	Adolescence
82. The need to develop confidence in myself and my abilities—self-confidence		√	√	√	√
83. The need to learn to control my emotions, desires, and actions without outside control—self-control			√	√	√
84. The need for positive perception of self—self-image			√	√	√
85. The need to develop an awareness of my own identity—self-identity			√	√	√
86. The need to develop positive thoughts of the mind—self-concept		√	√	√	√
87. The need to gain re-spect for self and un-derstand my value—self-respect			√	√	√
88. The need to gain confidence in myself and my own talents and abilities—self-awareness			√	√	√
89. The need to learn my true abilities and potential—self-discovery				√	√
90. The need to develop a purpose in life			√	√	√

continued

Need	Infant stage	Toddler stage	Early childhood	Middle childhood	Adolescence
91. The need to learn to make decisions according to my own mind or will without outside influence—self-determination				√	√
92. The need for a greater belief in my ability to complete a task successfully—self-efficiency			√	√	√
93. The need for a greater belief in my ability to continue a task once it has been started—self-sustainability			√	√	√
94. The need to love oneself—self-love			√	√	√
95. The need to control my desires and actions—self-discipline			√	√	√
96. The need to make decisions based on my own judgment—self-reliance				√	√
97. The need to gain confidence in myself and my abilities—self-assurance			√	√	√
98. The need to please parents and others that are important to me			√	√	√

continued

Need	Infant stage	Toddler stage	Early childhood	Middle childhood	Adolescence
99. The need to fulfill my aspirations and dreams—self-fulfillment					√
100. The need to be the best that I can be; to fulfill my potential and abilities in life—self-realization					√
101. The need to reach my full potential in life—the fulfillment of all my abilities and dreams—self-actualization					√

Figure 5.1   *101 Needs of children*

Reference

Children's Defense Fund. 1998. *The Children's Defense Fund's moments in America for black children.* Washington, D.C.: Children's Defense Fund.

African-American parents should develop in their children a divine self-expectancy concept. Parents should let their children know that they expect them to learn, make good grades, and become successful—that success is a birthright.

CHAPTER 6

What Parents Can Do to Help Their Children Become Brilliant and Successful

It is the dream of every parent to raise a smart and intelligent child. What can parents do to raise the intellectual and mental capabilities of their children? Are there things parents can do to help their children become brilliant and successful? These are some of the questions I encounter often in my counseling sessions with parents.

I have documented my research findings regarding the educational disadvantages for African-American children. Does this depressing and distressing information infer or conclude that African-American children are doomed for failure? The answer is no. It does provide important evidence that African-American parents must become active participants in their children's learning; and parents must continue to participate, through middle and high school, to help their children succeed.

African-American parents should develop in their children a divine self-expectancy concept. Parents should let their children know that they expect them to learn, make good grades and become successful—that success is a birthright. Parents' high expectations plus children's hard work equals greater academic success. If children are expected to learn, children will learn. Clear lines of responsibility should be established. Children should understand that it is their responsibility to master the academic skills necessary for them to succeed and that parents will be there to provide support and guidance.

Children are born with an innate resilience that allows them to overcome the negative environmental and social toxins they may encounter while growing up. This inborn capacity for resilience allows children to develop the following:

- Social competence; which includes qualities such as cooperativeness; the ability to evoke positive responses from others; empathy; effective communication skills; flexibility, including the ability to move between cultures; and a sense of humor.
- Problem-solving skills, which encompass the ability to think critically and creatively and to plan and to be resourceful in seeking help from others.
- A critical consciousness, perception, and awareness of the composition of oppression, which can include an alcoholic or abusive parent, an insensitive school, or a racist society. This consciousness will help children find ways to overcome the oppression.
- Autonomy, which is having a sense of one's own identity. It is also an ability to act independently and exert some control over one's environment, including a sense task mastery, internal parameters of control, and self-efficiency.
- A sense of purpose and belief in a bright future, which includes goals and directions, educational aspirations, achievement, motivation, hopefulness, optimism, and strong spiritual beliefs.

A large number of African-American children are growing up in families with single parents, poverty, crime, violence, and with family members who are abusive, mentally ill, alcoholic, drug abusers, incarcerated, and are involved in other criminal activities. Yet these children are able to overcome the risk, adversity, and barriers to success, and turn a life of high risk of academic failure and possible menace to society into a success.

Motivation

Parents' inspiration increases their children's aspiration.
—Will Horton

To help children become brilliant and successful, parents should take advantage of every opportunity to inspire and stimulate their children's creativity and learning abilities, and to create a desire and zest for learning. Parents should convey to their children an assurance of compassion, empathy, and understanding regardless of the children's successes or failures. The objective is to motivate children to want to succeed and to continue working toward success and to teach children that failure is never final. In fact, failure allows children to begin again. Parents should teach their children that failure is knowledge not yet learned. Elbert Hubbard, writing in *The Note Book,* says this about failure: "There is no failure except in no longer trying." Parents should teach their children the concepts babies use when learning to walk: If they fall while attempting to walk, they get up with a smile and try again.

Parents must teach and help their children to become self-reliant. Self-reliance is one of the most important guideposts for success. When parents inspire, stimulate, show enthusiasm, and communicate the value of learning by becoming involved in their children's learning and by setting high academic expectations, and when parents give children the support necessary to help strengthen their achievements, children's high school completion rates increase; they have better school attendance; and they are less likely to use drugs or become pregnant.

Using positive praises and actions plants the seeds of a positive self-concept. These are powerful motivators. They have the power to change a child's belief system. For children who have thought of themselves as being stupid and not loved, the use of positive praises and actions helps change the children's thought process and negative belief system. It also helps children feel they are special and have the ability to learn.

Inspiration

Parents can change their children's belief system and produce the desired thoughts and positive self-concepts by using daily positive praise and action concepts. Parents can inspire their children through positive parenting relationships that communicate positive words and actions, through high academic expectations, and by being positive role models. Parents should model the value of learning by letting their children see them learning—by reading a book, reading the newspaper, or reading to the child or asking the child to read to them.

Positive parental relationships will give children the motivation for wanting to succeed. Children will work harder and do things to please their parents because the children love and trust their parents by modeling their behavior. Modeling the expected behavior of children can be one of the most powerful tools parents use. Effective modeling develops an inspiring influence in children and stimulates creative thought and positive action. Effective modeling by parents creates in their children a strong desire and ambition to succeed. When parents set high expectations they are making the following statements to their children: Learning is important; you have the ability to be the best; you are special; you are a winner. I want you to be successful.

High expectations help children

- Build a positive self-image.
- Believe in their abilities, in themselves, and in their futures.
- Develop the critical resilience traits and building blocks of

positive self-esteem, self-assurance, self-efficiency, autonomy, and optimism.

Stimulation

What can parents do to stimulate children's natural curiosity to explore, discover, and learn? Children are born with a desire to learn, understand, and interact with the environment. Children also possess a curiosity about all of the conditions and influences that affect their surroundings. Children are born motivated. As an educator who works with young children, I have never seen a young child in preschool that was "unmotivated." Goethe says, "If children grew up according to early indications, we should have nothing but geniuses." The sad news is, as children grow older their motivation for learning diminishes. Their decreased zest for learning becomes a test for parents who sometimes feel disappointed and responsible for their children's lack of passion and interest in learning. According to the National Center for Education Statistics, in 1996 615,000 black students dropped out of school. The NCES reports that between 1972 and 1996 the dropout rate for blacks decreased to 17.6%. "Although the dropout rate for blacks decreased at a faster rate than that for whites, blacks were still more likely overall to drop out of school than their white peers. The status dropout rate for blacks was 13.0 compared to 7.3 for whites," according to the NCES. The Children's Defense Fund notes in its *Moments in America for Black Children* that "every 45 seconds of the school day a black child drops out."

These alarming statistics identify the need for African-American parents to find ways to motivate their children to stay in and succeed at school, and to stimulate and reawaken their natural curiosity to explore, discover, and learn. Thomas Jefferson suggested that "Every child must be encouraged to get as much education as he has the ability to take. We want this not only for his sake—but for the nation's sake." My suggestions are as follows:

- Help build in all African-American children a passion for learning. Parents must ensure that when their children enter the classroom, they are ready to learn. Many children go to school every day and answer "present" to the attendance roll call, but are cognitively absent from the pursuit of learning and academic excellence.
- Parents must model the behavior they expect from their children. Modeling by parents develops a pattern of expected behavior and establishes standards and guidelines of excellence. I like the quotation by James Baldwin. He says, "Children have never been very good at listening to their elders, but they have never failed to imitate them." Children learn by observing the words and actions of parents first, and other individuals in their environment later. Children will adopt the behavior that they are exposed to in their environment.
- Parents should reward their children for significant accomplishments and progress. Reward teaches expected behavior. By rewarding them, parents help their children build self-esteem, which will serve as a neutralizer to or counteraction to the negative effectiveness of failure and fear of failure.

Why Motivation Is Important to Children

Motivation can be best defined as a process that stimulates, incites, or affects a desired stimulation to action. Motivation in children is primarily concerned with learning and educational outcome. Motivation can be a factor in the behavior and discipline of children. The emphasis in this chapter is on motivation as it relates to learning. Motivation in children can be best defined as a process or act that stimulates, incites, or positively affects children's desire to succeed, to pursue excellence, and to work hard to excel.

There are two basic types of children's motivation—intrinsic and extrinsic. Intrinsically motivated children undertake academic challenges for their own sake and for the joy of learning. Intrinsically motivated children make learning decisions for their personal satisfaction and enjoyment. They make learning decisions according to their own mind or will, without outside influence. The learning of extrinsically motivated children is influenced by the objectives of receiving rewards or avoiding punishment from others. Rewards include getting good grades, stickers, and parent and teacher approval.

While both motivations can have successful academic and career outcomes, my preference is intrinsic motivation, which helps children become self-determined and independent. Extrinsic motivation can cause children to become dependent on others for approval and can create self-doubt and lower faith in oneself.

TELEVISION AND ITS EFFECT ON CHILDREN

Limit Television Viewing Time

Excessive television viewing has been found to be directly related to children's poor academic achievement and violent or overly aggressive behavior. When children watch more than two to three hours of television a day their overall academic achievement is low. The reason for this decline may be due to the fact that if children are watching excessive amounts of television they have less time for homework, reading, conversation with parents and other family members, and other intellectual activities, all of which build language skills.

According to an American Psychological Association task force report on television and American society, "by the time the average child—one who watches two to four hours of television daily—leaves elementary school, he or she will have witnessed at least 8000 murders and more than 100,000 other assorted acts of violence on television." A national study of television viewing habits of black children, conducted in 1994 by the National Center for Education Statistics, found that black children watch more television—six or more hours per day—than their white or Hispanic peers. That is four or more hours per day. The average African-American child, during the early important years of learning and intellectual development, is spending more time watching television than he or she is spending in formal academic pursuits.

Television Affects Children's Intellectual Development

When children spend excessive amounts of time watching television, they have less time for learning, homework, imagination, creativity, discovery, and creative play. TV affects children's ability to develop language skills because they are not able to engage in constructive conversations with parents and others while watching TV. Similarly, children watching television are not doing some of the most important activities that promote language skills, such as reading or being read to.

How Parents Can Help Their Children Learn from Television

Television can be an effective teaching vehicle for parents and an effective learning vehicle for children. If used effectively, television can stimulate children's imagination, and allow children to explore people and events in history, science, the arts, and nature. Children can discover while learning about geography, science, technology, and society. Children can learn about people who have made scientific contributions to our country such as inventors, educators, and explorers.

Set Time Limits for TV Viewing

Children should watch no more than one to two hours of educational television per day. When children watch more than two hours of television per day it has a negative effect on their academic performance.

Model TV Viewing Habits

Parents should model the expected TV viewing habits required of their children. Do not watch TV for long hours. Watch quality educational or entertainment programs. Do not watch programs that have a lot of violence and sex. Parents should never watch adult programs where children can hear or see them.

Plan a Weekly TV Viewing Schedule

Planned TV viewing helps children learn responsibility and enhances their self-image. They feel they are part of the family. Parents should encourage their children to watch a variety of programs that are appropriate for them. Use a newspaper or television guide to plan your TV viewing; this promotes reading skills.

Schedule a No-TV Day

No-TV days help children break the cycle and dependency on television. These days also provides parents an opportunity to participate and communicate with their children in alternative activities such as reading, conversation, play, educational games, and hobbies. Participate in activities that are important to your children.

Talk to Your Children about Television

Your children need your help to understand the powerful images that are being projected on television. Talk about the message the TV program is sending; about the violent content of the program and the effect it can have; and about conflict resolutions. Ask your children for their opinion on how to handle the portrayed problem differently.

By modeling and monitoring their children's TV viewing habits, parents can have a powerful influence in ensuring that television is a positive conduit for learning. When parents are involved with their children's TV viewing—planning, watching it with them, explaining program images, and asking for their children's view—the children's language and writing skills improve.

Reference

Children's Defense Fund. 1998. *The Children's Defense Fund's moments in America for black children.* Washington, D.C.: Children's Defense Fund.

The most important thing parents can do to awaken and encourage the imagination and curiosity of their children is to **BECOME INVOLVED** *in their children's education, at home before they start school. And when the children start school, parents must* **STAY INVOLVED**.

CHAPTER 7

Steps to Make Your Children Honor Roll Students

T
eaching children to learn and succeed in school can be a wonderful experience for the whole family. Children are born with five natural resources for learning: an unlimited imagination, creativity, curiosity, a desire to discover, and a desire to learn. As a parent you can awaken these innate abilities already formed in your child's brain, and create a lifelong joy for learning by encouraging your child's imagination, curiosity, and affection for learning. I recommend reading Thomas Armstrong's book, *Awakening Your Child's Natural Genius,* in which he talks about the role parents can play in enhancing the curiosity, creativity, and learning ability of children.

Parents can encourage their children's curiosity and joy of learning and help their children become honor roll students by turning that "joy of learning" into a lifelong "passion for learning."

All children, regardless of circumstance, have the ability to succeed in school and in life—to realize the American Dream. What can African-American parents do to help their children succeed? What can parents do to awaken and encourage the imagination and curiosity of their children? The answer is very simple. The most important thing parents can do is **BECOME INVOLVED** in their children's education, at home, before they start school. And when the children start school, parents must **STAY INVOLVED.**

LEARNING BEGINS AT HOME

Parents are their children's first teacher. Parents can have a profound influence on children's cognitive and intellectual development. Positive parenting influences contribute to a higher intelligence quotient (IQ) and academic achievement. Parents must practice using positive praises and actions. What parents say and do helps teach children their expected behavior and academic learning objectives. Using positive praises and actions will help develop self-esteem and self-worth, which will help children excel in school and later in life.

The road to academic success begins in the home, with a safe, secure, and healthy environment; caring and loving relationships; and positive parental guidance. Research shows that what parents do to help their children learn is more important to academic success than how rich or poor parents are or how much education parents have. "What we do in the home is what we end up seeing out on the streets in one way or another," says psychologist Madeleine Gomez.

Ten Things Parents Can Do in the Home to Help Their Children Learn

1. Communicate the value of learning by displaying books, magazines, and newspapers in various rooms of the home. Model the value of learning by letting your children see you read. Build a library in the home. Inexpensive books can be purchased from dollar stores and garage sales.
2. Read aloud to your children. Reading promotes language development and enhances reading readiness skills.
3. Buy a supply of crayons, pencils, washable markers, and paper for writing practice.

4. Teach self-help skills, such as putting on clothes, washing hands, and proper hygiene. Teach children to become independent. Teach responsibility by letting them help clean their room.

5. Give children a quiet study space with their own desk and chair, if possible. If you do not have the space, any quiet room will be sufficient.

6. Turn off all televisions and competing media. Children sometimes like to use the radio as background music; this is okay. Find out what works best for your children. Some children need total quietness to study and concentrate. Some children study best with music in the background. Establish specific times for study and homework and be consistent. Children want and need consistency.

7. Set limits on TV time and types of programs viewed. Watch TV with your children and discuss the content and programs you do not like. Give reasons such as, "This show has too much violence," or "This show does not promote racial harmony."

8. Establish clear and consistent rules for children such as bedtime hour, nutrition and meal schedules, and chores and household responsibilities. Children want and need structure in their lives.

9. Set learning goals for your children. For example: When my child enters preschool she will know her colors and shapes or will be able to sing the ABC song. An excellent learning goal may be: When my child completes high school he will have achieved high academic standards by taking advanced algebra, calculus, biology, chemistry, and physics and by learning a foreign language.

10. Encourage your children's efforts and accomplishments. Expect your children to learn and to succeed in school and in life. Impel and stimulate the inherent inclination of your children's desire to learn. Nurture your children's creativity and zeal to explore and discover.

WHAT PARENTS CAN DO TO HELP THEIR CHILDREN SUCCEED IN SCHOOL

Parents that make effective use of the time their children spend at home and in preschool have built a strong educational foundation to help their children become successful. A good quality preschool is one of the most important educational assets contributing to African-American children's success. In elementary school, parents should put a greater focus on the school's curriculum, educational objectives, and standards. Curriculum is important because success outcomes in one course determine success outcomes in the next course. Many courses in elementary and high school follow a specific sequence. Students must complete algebra and trigonometry before they can study calculus.

The most important thing is for parents to be involved. Here are seven things parents can do at school to help their children succeed.

1. Meet your children's teachers, and give them your home telephone number. Doing this sends a message to the teachers and the children that you value education.

   - Find out the learning objectives for important subjects like English, math, science, and history.
   - Ask if African-American history will be taught.
   - Ask the teachers if homework will be required.
   - If yes, ask: What is your policy and how often do you assign homework?
   - Ask how students are tested.
   - Ask how the teachers handle individual differences in children's learning abilities.
   - Ask if there is anything that you can do to help your child succeed in school.

2. Become a partner in your children's learning by developing a parent/teacher partnership. Parent participation in children's learning is a key ingredient for success in

school. Experience and research suggest that when parents participate, children learn.

3. Discuss and review your children's homework. Homework provides an excellent opportunity for parents to be involved in their children's education and to monitor their children's progress. I am often asked by parents in some of my workshops, What are the benefits of homework? I first establish the fact that homework is very important to learning. Some of the benefits of homework are listed below. Homework helps children to

- Practice and review the learning concepts or subjects taught in class.
- Prepare for the next day's learning concepts or subjects.
- Gain greater knowledge of the subject through independent exploration and research.
- Learn about valuable resources, such as libraries, the World Wide Web, computers, and encyclopedias.
- Acquire self-discipline, responsibility, and the ability to work independently.
- Foster a love of learning, to make learning fun in school and to help improve children's academic achievement. Research has found that from middle school on, students who complete more homework score better on standardized tests and earn better grades, on the average, than students who do less homework.

4. Participate in parent/teacher conferences, meetings, and workshops held by the school. The children's father should be included in all school programs. The importance of fathers' involvement in child rearing and family/school programs is usually disregarded. Research has found that when fathers are involved with their children, their social, emotional, and cognitive skills are enhanced. The father's role will be discussed in detail in chapter 9.

5. Promote healthy eating habits and ensure that your children eat balanced and nutritious meals each day. There is

a direct link between nutrition and children's ability to learn. Deborah Rees, a licensed dietician and regional coordinator for the Illinois Nutrition Education and Training program, says,

> Research shows that nutrition plays a key role in both the cognitive development of children and in their school performance. Two of the more common threats to intellectual development of children are under nutrition and iron deficiency/anemia. Chronically undernourished children score lower on achievement tests and studies show that undernourished children are also more likely to get sick, miss school, and then fall behind because of it. Even moderate under nutrition such as just skipping breakfast has been found to affect the child's ability to complete problem-solving tests in school. Even on the attention span of children in the classroom—if children are thinking about their next meal they are not concentrating on what they are doing in the classroom. Marie Stewart, a retired kindergarten and early childhood educator with over 30 years of teaching experience, concurs with the research that shows that nutrition affects students' ability to learn. Stewart made the following observations regarding her students: "When children came to my class hungry they did not pay attention, they did not respond to the class activities. They were not with it. They were out of it."

6. Encourage your children to learn a second language. Research suggests that when children learn a second language their school performance, creativity, and problem-solving skills are improved. Children who learn a foreign language have been found to score statistically higher on standardized tests. With our new global society, students' knowledge of a foreign language will increase their career opportunities.
7. Set high standards and academic excellence for your children and encourage them to be the best that they can be.

Too many African-American children are not meeting the standards that will prepare them for the challenges of our new global society. As a people, we do not expect enough of our children. High standards and expectations are essential motivators for learning. These motivators help instill in children the value of learning and hard work. To meet the challenges African-American children will face in the new millennium and prepare them for the new technological advancements and opportunities in our global society, it is necessary for African-American children to take more advanced mathematics courses such as algebra II, trigonometry, analysis/precalculus, and calculus; and more advanced courses in biology, chemistry, and physics.

There is some good news about African-American student achievement. Over the last two decades African-American children have begun to close the large gap in academic achievement between black and white children. According to the National Center for Education Statistics,

> The large gap in achievement between whites and African-Americans has narrowed in mathematics and science. Although the gap was still large in 1994, the mathematics proficiency scores for 17-year-old white students increased only 2 scale points between 1973–1974 from 310 to 312, and the scores for African-Americans increased 16 scale points, from 270 to 286. (See Tables 7.1–7.4 for details.)

ACADEMIC ACHIEVEMENT IN AFRICAN-AMERICAN CHILDREN

The National Center for Education Statistics (NCES) data in Tables 7.5 and 7.6 show that the reading gap between white and African-American students is decreasing. One of the purposes of this book is to provide African-American parents with guide-

Table 7.1. Average mathematics proficiency (scale score) by race/ethnicity and age: 1973.

	Score at age 9	Score at age 13	Score at age 17
Whites	225	274	310
African-Americans	190	228	270
Difference in scale scores	35	46	40

Table 7.2. Average mathematics proficiency (scale score) by race/ethnicity and age: 1994.

	Score at age 9	Score at age 13	Score at age 17
Whites	237	281	312
African-Americans	212	252	286
Difference in scale scores	25	29	26

Note: The matematics proficiency scale ranges from 0 to 500.

Level 150: Simple arithmetic facts

Level 200: Beginning skills and understandings

Level 250: Numerical operations and beginning problem solving

Level 300: Moderately complex procedures and reasoning

level 350: Multi-step problem solving and algebra

Source: National Center for Education Statistics. Recalculated to show specific comparisons.

Table 7.3. Average science proficiency (scale score) by race/ethnicity and age: 1970.

	Score at age 9	Score at age 13	Score at age 17
Whites	236	263	312
African-Americans	179	215	258
Difference in scale scores	57	48	54

Note: The science proficiency scale ranges from 0 to 500.

Level 150: Knows everyday science facts.

Level 200: Understands simple scientific principles.

Level 250: Applies general scientific information.

Level 300: Analyzes scientific procedures and data.

Level 350: Integrates specialized scientific information.

Source: National Center for Education Statistics. Recalculated to show specific comparisons.

Table 7.4. Average science proficiency (scale score) by race/ethnicity and age: 1994.

	Score at age 9	Score at age 13	Score at age 17
Whites	240	267	306
African-Americans	201	224	257
Difference in scale scores	39	43	49

Note: The science proficiency scale ranges from 0 to 500.

Level 150: Knows everyday science facts.

Level 200: Understands simple scientific principles.

Level 250: Applies general scientific information.

Level 300: Analyzes scientific procedures and data.

Level 350: Integrates specialized scientific information.

Source: National Center for Education Statistics. Recalculated to show specific comparisons.

Table 7.5. Average reading proficiency (scale score) by race/ethnicity and age: 1971.

	Score at age 9	Score at age 13	Score at age 17
Whites	214	261	291
African-Americans	170	222	239
Difference in scale scores	44	39	52

Table 7.6. Average reading proficiency (scale score) by race/ethnicity and age: 1994.

	Score at age 9	Score at age 13	Score at age 17
Whites	218	265	296
African-Americans	185	234	266
Difference in scale scores	33	31	30

Note: The reading proficiency scale ranges from 0 to 500.

Level 150: Simple, discrete reading tasks.

Level 200: Partial skills and understanding.

Level 250: Interrelates ideas and makes generalizations.

Level 300: Understands complicated information.

Level 350: Learns from speicalized reading materials.

Source: National Center for Education Statistics. Recalculated to show specific comparisons.

posts that will help to eliminate this gap. African-American parents are on the right track and must continue to work with their children to pursue academic excellence.

The gap in academic achievement between African-American children and white children will be annihilated if the success strategies suggested in this book are implemented in every home. Many African-American homes are already applying these strategies—you must continue to participate and implement them to eliminate this gap in academic achievement.

According to Wendy M. William and Stephen J. Ceci, two experts in intelligence testing at Cornell University, "The intelligence test scores of whites compared to African-Americans are not growing wider, as some reports are being made in the academic and research circles." Harvard University psychologist Richard J. Herrnstein and political scientist Charles Murray wrote a book called *The Bell Curve: Intelligence and Class Structure in American Life.* Herrnstein and Bell suggest the old racial stereotype that African-Americans are less intelligent than whites, and this ethnic gap in IQ test scores may be related to genes. They are using the research data that show that black children score about 15 points lower on standard IQ tests than white children.

This book will not attempt to get into *The Bell Curve* debate. For parents who would like to read more about this issue I suggest reading, *The Bell Curve Wars, Race Intelligence,* and *The Future of America,* edited by Steven Fraser.

The objective of this book is to give African-American parents tools and guideposts they can use to help their children become successful and to help raise the IQ and academic achievement levels of their children. It is from my experience and beliefs, which are being outlined in this book, that parents can raise the intellectual and cognitive abilities of African-American children by becoming involved in their children's educational development at an early age, and continue through middle school, high school, and postsecondary school.

The IQ and academic achievement gaps that exist between African-American children and white children exist because many African-American parents do not take advantage of the learning curve and windows of opportunity for cognitive development between the ages of zero and three. Recent research on brain development and the critical first three years of a child's life suggest that parents can increase their children's IQ by 20 points in the first three years, and can reduce mental retardation by up to 50 percent, by stimulating the brain. Parents can help raise their children's IQ and improve their learning abilities by creating a positive and stimulating learning environment.

Further research shows that there is a direct relationship between nutrition and learning. Good nutrition has been found to help a child's brain to develop. Nutrition and learning are interrelated. Children's ability to learn and the effect nutrition has on IQ development are much more important to children's development than many parents realize. Food and its relationship to learning can be put in two different categories—food for the body and food for the mind. Food for the body can be defined as nourishment that stimulates growth, development, and good health. Food for the mind can be defined as nourishment that stimulates intellectual development and mental capabilities. Cognitive abilities and IQ are not inherited but are developed. Factors such as the child's environment, socioeconomic status, and the role of the family can contribute to a child having a lower or higher IQ. A study by researchers at Columbia and Northwestern Universities suggests "that poverty and early learning opportunities not race account for the gap in IQ scores between African-Americans and whites."

GUIDEPOSTS FOR SUCCESS: PARENTS—TAKE 60 MINUTES EACH DAY TO HELP YOUR CHILDREN BUILD THE SKILLS NECESSARY FOR SUCCESS

1. <u>TAKE 10</u> minutes to <u>**TALK**</u> to your children. Talking to your children lets them know that you are concerned and care about them. Talking helps to build trust and bonds between parents and children. Talk about their learning experiences of the day, or successes or problems they may have.

2. <u>TAKE 10</u> minutes to <u>**LISTEN**</u> to your children. By listening carefully, parents are modeling good listening skills required of their children. Listening is one of the primary means of interacting with children on a personal basis. Most parents talk at or with their children but do not listen to them. Effective listening practices allow parents to find out what's on a child's mind and what she or he understands or doesn't understand. Effective listening gives parents feedback on their children's cognitive abilities. Parents can help children to become more self-determined by asking open-ended questions that will allow the children to provide the answer to problems they may have.

3. <u>TAKE 10</u> minutes to <u>**READ**</u> to your children or have your children read to you. As children become older, encourage them to read at least 30 minutes each day. Reading aloud helps your children develop language and reading skills, builds vocabulary, and creates a lifelong love for learning.

4. <u>TAKE 10</u> minutes to <u>**ENCOURAGE**</u> your children. Encourage your children through positive words and actions. Use the positive praises and actions approach discussed earlier. Encourage your children to want to learn and succeed—to be the best that they can be. Help your children develop positive self-esteem and self-concept. Children's self-esteem grows with encouragement and positive parental intervention.

5. <u>TAKE 10</u> minutes to <u>**PLAY**</u> with your children. Play helps to stimulate your children's imagination and creativity. Play helps to expand your children's curiosity, explore their senses, and learn about the environment and how the world works. Play is important to young children's development and health. Play is an effective learning tool for children. Have you ever seen a child who did not like to play?

6. <u>TAKE 10</u> minutes to <u>**EXPRESS LOVE**</u> to your children. Children need the assurance of your love every day. One of the most significant needs of a child is the need to feel

loved. There are many ways parents can express their love for their children.

- Affectionate love is shown by touching, hugging, holding, and kissing your children. The objective of expressing love is to build trust, show love and concern, and to become more closely connected—to bond with your children.
- Provide a safe and healthy environment. Children learn best when they feel protected and secure.
- Provide your children with stable relationships. Children need stable relationships in their lives to serve as a buffer against the negative environment and social toxins they may encounter in the form of violence, crime, poverty, racism, and other societal ills.

In elementary school, parents should focus on the school's curriculum, educational objective and standards. Curriculum is important because success outcomes in one course determine success outcomes in the next course. Many courses in elementary and high school follow a specific sequence.

The growing needs of African-American children, the diversity of families, and the growing number of working parents increase the need to develop a support network for African-American children. The support network does not release parents from their basic responsibility—the critical job of providing the terra firma and milieu for their children to live by, such as a positive self-identity, morals, responsibility, respect for life, and character.

CHAPTER 8

Building a Support Network
and Instilling Morals and Values

There is an old African proverb that states, "It takes a village to raise a child." This proverb remains true today. While the composition of the village has changed, the premise of the proverb has germane meaning.

Many African-American children face serious social, cultural, and economic challenges to their development and are at high risk of academic and professional failure. Fifty percent of African-American children live in poverty. African-American children are also highly likely to

- Drop out of school.
- Face a disorderly learning environment.
- Experience early school problems.
- Have exposure to and experience violence.
- Live with a single parent.
- Attend a high-poverty school.
- Have a teacher with negative attitudes and low expectations of students.

Black male youths face even greater challenges and are at even higher risks of failure in school and in life. Young black males are highly likely to

- Experience violent crimes at significantly higher rates than for other racial groups.
- Be arrested for a violent crime.
- Be approached to join a street gang.
- Drop out of school.
- Score lower on achievement tests.
- Be suspended from school more frequently and for longer periods of time than other student groups.
- Be placed in special education classes for the mentally retarded and for students with learning disabilities.
- Be bypassed for special education classes for gifted and talented students.
- Have a teacher who expects students to have low academic achievement and who expects students to experience learning and behavior problems.

As parents, you need the support of the village to help your children overcome the barriers to academic and professional success—to realize the American Dream. The village has been given a new name—your support network. The support network should include members of your immediate family; your extended family and friends; school personnel, including teachers; your church and/or divine house of worship; ministers and religious leaders; and community organizations.

WHY THE NEED FOR A SUPPORT NETWORK?

Today's African-American families are more diverse and nontraditional. They are made up of dual-parent families; an increasing number of single parent families; single-career families; dual-career families; mother-custody families; father-custody families; joint-custody families; foster parent families; working mother and father families; working single mother families; and working single father families. The growing needs of African-American children, the diversity of families, and the growing number of working parents increase the need to develop a support network for African-American children. The support network does not release parents from their basic responsibility—the critical job of providing the terra firma and milieu for their children to live by, such as a positive self-identity, morals, responsibility, respect for life, and character.

INSTILLING MORALS AND CHARACTER VALUES

In addition to self-esteem and the need to establish a positive self-concept in African-American children, there is the need for moral and character development. If African-American children are going to be able to overcome the challenges and obstacles to academic and career success, they must have highly developed principles in morals and character. These are subjects that are not frequently discussed in many African-American families. Not only do they need to be discussed at every opportunity, but they must also become a part of the African-American parents' guideposts for success. I like John Morley's view of character. He said: "No man can climb out beyond the limitations of his own character." If African-American children are going to overcome the impediments to success, they must develop their character, moral perception, and self-determination.

Like most parents, you have dreams for your children. You want them to be successful in life. Dr. Martin Luther King, Jr. had a dream for his children and for the country. In his speech at the Lincoln Memorial in Washington, D.C. on August 28, 1966, King shared his dream with the world.

> I have a dream that one day this nation will rise up and live out the true meaning of its creed: "We hold these truths to be self-evident that all men are created equal." . . . I have a dream that my four little children will one day live in a nation where they will not be judged by the color of their skin but by the content of their character. I have a dream today.

What are your dreams for your children? What are you going to do to counter the academic and social problems facing African-American children? The following guideposts for teaching and building children's character and moral perception can be useful to parents in their efforts to develop the whole child— to ensure that your children succeed in school and in life. It is the parents' role to teach and help children become responsible for their achievement and success—and to encourage, support, and expect success.

One of the first steps in teaching character and morals to children is for parents to mirror their teachings by example. Some examples for mirroring are as follows:

- Respect the rights of your child. (Moral lesson: Right)
- Do not abuse your child. Use positive discipline. (Moral lesson: Right)
- Yelling at your child. (Moral lesson: Wrong)

Earl James McGrath said, "The best way to teach our young people the meaning of our democratic freedoms is to demonstrate, by our example, that we have mastered the 'three Rs' of citizenship—Rights, Respect, and Responsibility." Children need some standards or guideposts to live by in order to relate to and make concrete decisions between right and wrong; to establish appropriate behaviors; and to develop mental habits and traits that will help them become responsible adults. If parents help their children build strong characters, they will grow up to be successful men and women.

MORAL AND CHARACTER DEVELOPMENT GUIDEPOSTS TO LIVE BY

Responsibility

Parents should help their children to learn to become accountable for their behavior and responsible for their academic achievement and success. Children should be responsible for the successful and timely completion and return of homework and school projects; for making good grades; for being organized; and for helping with chores in the home. Parents should plant the seeds of positive expectations in children by communicating the value of success—that they are expected to succeed. Responsibility is one of the most important characters for success. "The price of greatness is responsibility," said Winston Churchill.

Respect

Children should have high regard, honor, and esteem for themselves, and should express feelings of honor and esteem for others. Children should show consideration and respect for parents, teachers, elders, property, rules, and the law. Children should develop a personality trait based on courtesy and politeness. They should routinely use terms such as "please," "thank you," "excuse me," "May I help you?" Confucius asked, "Without feelings of respect, what is there to distinguish men from beasts?"

Honesty

Honesty is one of the most commendable character traits children can learn. Honesty helps children gain confidence and trust from others. Children should be taught honesty is the best policy and to be honest with parents, self, friends, teachers, and society. John Ruskin said, "To make your children capable of honesty is the beginning of education."

Hard Work

Nothing can substitute for the value of hard work; however, hard work can substitute for not being born with wealth. Hard work can help many African-American children, who are living in poverty and exposed to other societal ills, to succeed in school and in life. Anything that has significant value such as a good education and a good career requires hard work. Enthusiasm, persistence, determination, and hard work are formulas for success. President Harry S. Truman said, "I found that the men and women who got to the top were those who did the jobs they had in hand, with everything they had of energy and enthusiasm and hard work."

Determination

A firm belief system that they are expected to succeed should be established in children's mental concepts. From this system, a firmness of purpose and resolution should be the driving force to the pursuit of high achievement and excellence. "Decision and determination are the engineer and fireman of our train to opportunity and success," noted Burt Lawlor. Many African-American children are living in poverty, exposed to violence, experiencing violence, being mentally and physically neglected and abused, and have people close to them, whom they trust and respect, who believe that they are going to fail. These children can succeed in school and in life if they are determined. Parents must help their children build the character of determination—to never, never, never give up. I use the following never-give-up affirmations in some of my parenting lectures and workshops.

I Will Never Give Up
- I may be poor but I will never give up.
- I may be on welfare but I will never give up.
- I may have holes in my shoes but I will never give up.
- I may not have designer clothes but I will never give up.
- I may not have people who love me but I will never give up.
- I may have friends and love ones who expect me to fail but I will never give up.
- I will never give up—because I am special—I am unique—I am a winner—you see. I'm a child of God—and God only makes winners, that's why—I will never—never—never give up.

When children have a definite purpose such as making good grades or making the honor roll they are determined they will succeed. When problems arise the parents' wisdom should be shared with the children to encourage determination. I like the wisdom of this poem. The author is unknown.

Don't Quit

When things go wrong, as they sometimes will,
When the road you're trudging seems all up hill,
When care is pressing you down a bit,
Rest, if you must—but don't you quit.
Often the goal is nearer than it seems
to a faint and faltering man.
Often the struggler has given up,
When he might have captured the victor's cup.

Dependability

All parents want their children to be independent and self-sufficient and to be able to trust them. One of the most important connections between trust and dependability is what children say in relations to what children do. Words are powerful for children too, and children must be taught the importance of keeping their word. I grew up in a large family in a small community. My family taught me the value of "the word"—and the importance of keeping a promise. "Your word," as my mother would say, "is your bond." We were taught that your word should be considered as a binding obligation, agreement, or contract. In our small community a handshake was used as an agreement or contract. When children give true meaning to words by doing what they say they are going to do, this builds trust with parents and others. The value of the word is better explained in Deuteronomy 30:14, "But the word is very near you, in your mouth and in your heart, that you may do it." (NKJV)

Discipline

One of the most influential factors that affects children's learning is discipline. It is the parents' responsibility to help their children learn the acceptable and expected conduct for self-discipline and self-control. Children are not born with self-discipline; they must learn it. Children should learn the value of respect, for self and others. Children should start school ready to obey the school's rules, study hard, complete assignments and homework, and become successful in school.

Temperance in behavior, conflict resolution, and delayed gratification should be included in all discipline training. Children who have good discipline and respect for teachers have high academic success in school. A strong motivation for teaching delayed gratification is income potential. The difference in lifetime earning between a high school dropout and a college graduate is over $1 million.

Courage

Many African-American children will face overwhelming problems and challenges in their environment that will interfere with their academic achievement and future career success. African-American children will need resilience to overcome many of the academic and career-threatening challenges they will face in life. The character trait courage, if highly developed in children, will help give them resilience to overcome these dangers. Dorothy Thompson said:

> Courage, it would seem, is nothing less than the power to overcome danger, misfortune, fear, injustice, while continuing to affirm inwardly that life with all its sorrows is good; that everything is meaningful even if in a sense beyond our understanding; and that there is always tomorrow.

Compassion

The character compassion can best be defined as a regard for another person's pain, suffering, and trouble, and a desire to help. Compassion has two fields of view—sympathy and empathy.

Sympathy is the perception and understanding of a person's emotions, thoughts, and feelings in which you understand, approve, and agree with them. The counselor is expressing sympathy in the following exchange.

PARENT: I participate in my child's learning because I feel that it is important for parents to participate.

COUNSELOR: I understand and agree with you.

Parents can help their children learn compassion by teaching them compassion—not criticizing them. Alexander Pope said, "Teach me to feel another's woe, to hide the fault I see." If we teach and value compassion, children will become more compassionate.

Empathy is the perception and understanding of a person's emotions, thoughts, and feelings, and you being able to understand them, although you may not agree with them. The counselor is demonstrating empathy in the following exchange.

PARENT: I use corporal punishment often to teach my child discipline.

COUNSELOR: I understand the need for discipline in your child but I do not believe that corporal punishment is the best way to teach a child discipline.

Many African-American children do not have respect for or value life because they lack the character trait compassion. You can help build compassion in your children's daily life by modeling compassion in your child-rearing techniques, by expressing love, by listening, respecting, sharing, and by helping others.

Loyalty

The development of loyalty in children is a necessary ingredient to being faithful and adhering to the standards of excellence in both academic and career pursuits. Parents expect children to be loyal to their family—their foundation and support; to their teachers and school; and to themselves. Students should be encouraged to develop a passion for learning and to look for a greater purpose in life—an opportunity to make a contribution to a cause or to the community, such as volunteering to feed the hungry or tutoring needy students or adults. Cyril Connolly noted, "When young we are faithful to individuals, when older we grow more loyal to situations and to types."

Love

Love is one of the greatest gifts parents can give to their children. Love is a foundational building block to children's well-being and success. When children develop trust and feel loved by parents and others that are important and responsible for them, children will express love to others.

Wisdom from the Bible teaches us that "Love must be sincere. Hate what is evil; cling to what is good. Be devoted to one another in brotherly love. Honor one another above yourselves" (Romans 12: 9–10) (NIV). Children should love themselves, and should express unconditional love to their parents, caregivers, teachers, family, and friends. Henry Miller said, "The one thing we can never get enough of is love. And the one thing we never give enough of is love."

Psychologists have found that when fathers are involved with their children's development, their social, emotional, and cognitive skills are enhanced.

CHAPTER 9

The Influence Factors: Parents Are Their Children's First Teacher

Thirty years of educational research validates the fact that parents' involvement in their children's education has the most powerful influence on children's achievement in school. When parents participate in their children's education in positive ways, children earn higher grades, score higher on tests, have better school attendance, have a more positive attitude about and complete more homework, are less likely to drop out of school, have a more positive attitude, have a more positive behavior, graduate from high school at higher rates, and are more likely to enroll in college than children whose parents are less involved in their children's education. Parent involvement and participation in their children's learning is of greater significance to the children's academic success than the parents' socioeconomic background. *Successful parenting, regardless of race, income, or social environment, has the ability to ensure the educational success of children.*

Interest and participation in their children's education have been found to be primary motivators. Parents' participation improves their children's attitude and class performance, increases their academic achievement, and closely bonds the children to their parents.

Parenting can be one of the most rewarding experiences of a

lifetime. As a parent, I can find no other significant accomplishment in my professional life that exceeds the joy and satisfaction of raising a responsible, productive, and happy son. No other experience has brought me more peace, happiness, joy, pride, and sense of accomplishment. The following guideposts for successful parenting can be used by African-American parents to help their children develop highly effective techniques for success.

GUIDEPOSTS FOR SUCCESSFUL PARENTING

Teach Your Children the Significance and Value of Education

The job market is changing by leaps and bounds because of the burgeoning growth of technology and opportunities in foreign markets. A great number of jobs now require more than a high school diploma and the ability to use technology in the new global economy. Jobs in the technology-driven twenty-first century will require higher skills in science and mathematics. Some jobs will require knowledge of a second language. Children should be taught that the benefit of an education is the best long-term investment they can make in themselves. According to the U.S. Census Bureau, the difference in lifetime earning between a student who did not graduate from high school and one who did is over $200,000. The difference in lifetime earnings between a student who received a bachelors degree or more and a high school dropout is over $1 million. Parents must instill in their children a lifelong joy for learning.

Foster a Passion for Learning

Parents must help their children develop an insatiable desire for the value of learning. Learning is a lifelong process. Children must develop the ability to continue to learn and update their skills and to change to meet the new technological advances that will occur in the new millennium.

Develop High Expectations and Academic Standards

If parents expect their children to learn and excel, they will learn and excel. Children learn best when they are challenged by high expectations and standards.

Believe in Your Children

Parents must have hope and faith in their children's ability to learn and be successful. Every child in every family regardless of socioeconomic background has the ability to succeed in school and in life. Believe that your children will succeed.

Help Develop Positive Self-Identity

Parents must help their children develop a positive self-identity. Children with high self-esteem and a positive self-identity appear to be happy, are likely to enjoy learning, learn easily, and are successful in school.

Encourage Ethnic Pride

Parents must teach their children to be proud of their heritage. Teaching and developing ethnic pride helps children to better understand their culture, social structure, and birthrights, and helps to develop a self-identity in the pursuit of finding the ideal self.

Teach Values

Children look to parents for guidance and direction in life. Parents must teach their children the difference between appropriate and inappropriate behavior in order for the children to understand the behavior parents expect. It is the parents' responsibility to develop a value system that teaches children principles, goals, and standards to live by. Parents must teach the value of hard work—that children may have to study and work hard but the rewards are worth it in the form of higher grades and career success. Children want and respond better to organized family structure and continuity in family rules. Parents must create an environment based on trust, respect, honesty, courage, love, dependability, responsibility, friendship, and loyalty.

Foster Spiritual Values

Spiritual values help children to learn values to live by and to better understand their purpose in life and their reason for being. Spiritual values help build children's self-esteem and self-assurance by allowing children to reach out to a higher being, to better cope with life's problems and challenges. According to clinical psychologist Madeleine Gomez,

> Spirituality does, in part, serve as a certain internal sense of peace that translates into a positive self-esteem for the child. It can be a spirituality that is formal such as religion or a spirituality that is not so formal but still gives an internal code of ethics and values that children can fall back on despite whatever chaos that is going on in the real world.

Communicate With Your Children

Parents must communicate to their children and must express love, enthusiasm, and respect for the needs, wants, and rights of their children. Parents should communicate an optimistic and positive attitude in relation to all activities involving their children. Parents should talk and listen to their children, should use positive words, and should model positive expected behaviors.

Monitor Your Children's Progress

Parents should monitor the progress of their children's development at home and at school. Parents can reward progress and significant accomplishments. My experience in working with children and the latest research show that when parents express interest in, and participate in their children's education, their opportunities for academic success are greatly enhanced. Parents should watch their children's sleep habits to ensure that they get plenty of rest each night and are ready to learn when they go to school.

Express Love

Parents must express love to their children, assuring them through words and actions of the parents' love. Children need the assurance of parental love every day. When you hug, kiss, hold, or cuddle your children it reassures them that you love them. Parents should make it a daily practice of expressing love to their children. Dr. Benjamin Spock said, "Love is a parent's most powerful tool—and gift—for raising happy, loving, and well-adjusted children." Positive words and actions help to express love, interest, and concern. One of the most necessary and important needs of children is the need to feel loved. When children are loved their self-concept is enhanced.

Spend Time with Your Children

The amount of time parents spend with their children is less important than how parents spend the time (the qualitative time versus quantitative time argument). An example of quantitative time is:

A father is in the living room watching television, and his son is also in the room. The son is attempting to talk to the father but the father's primary attention is on the football game. He gives his son secondary attention with quick answers such as "Uh-huh," "Yes," and "No."

An example of qualitative time is:

Same scenario, except that the father turns off the television and any other competing media and reads a book or discusses the child's learning experiences he had at school. The father also explores his son's questions and offers his insights on those questions.

It pays to spend time with your children. The sheriff of Cook County jail in Illinois has a poster that he sends to schools each year during a crime prevention campaign. I like the poster very much; it is creative and makes a valuable statement. The poster states, "Parents spend time with your child—If you don't I will." I give parents basically the same theme when I counsel them at my early childhood development center and during my lectures and workshops. My advice to parents is: "The time you spend with your child now will pay dividends later when your child starts college in the form of academic scholarships and tuition saved. Furthermore, you can spend time now with your child or money later on your child."

Recognize the Value of Your Involvement

Parents must recognize the value of their involvement and how it will influence and shape their children's personality. Parents have the most influence on their children's learning and development. Research constantly highlights the power of the parents. When parents are involved in their children's education the results are always positive. Parental involvement can make children become productive members of society.

Establish Close Contact with Your Children

Parents should have a positive, warm, and devoted relationship with their children. Close contact with parents helps children build trust and self-esteem. Establishing close contact will open the lines of communication between parents and children. Open and honest communication allows children the freedom to talk about problems they may encounter. Developing this special relationship between parent and child requires patience, understanding, time, and commitment, but it is most rewarding for both parent and child. These factors will become very significant to children during adolescence when they begin to make major decisions about friends, dating, sex, drugs, college, and other critical decisions.

Provide a Safety Net

The home should be the safety net for children to buffer them from society's negative elements, such as violence, crime, and racism. Parents should make the home as safe and secure as possible. The home should also be peaceful and inviting and should encourage family unity. Parents must monitor their own disagreements, verbal fights, and inappropriate words with each other. Parents must also monitor their complaints and reprimands to their children. You do not want your home to become satiated with negative self-fulfilling forces.

Accentuate the Positive

There is no greater skill you can give your children than a positive self-concept. Parents must practice using positive praises and actions. Parents must avoid using sexist words, racist words, diminutive names, and negative nicknames, because these words help children to form a negative belief system about themselves.

Provide Superior Nutrition

Nutrition affects children's ability to learn. When children are hungry or under nourished, they become irritable, apathetic, and lethargic, and have difficulty learning. Parents should pay close attention to the nutritional needs of their children, making sure that they receive well-balanced meals to meet their dietary requirements.

Provide Opportunities for Growth

Parents need to allow room for age-appropriate independence and growth development. Some African-American parents use an authoritarian parenting style. This style imposes so many overly restrictive rules and control limits that children never develop the ability to make decisions and become independent. It is important that parents give their children the opportunity to learn responsibility, become independent, and grow developmentally.

Play with Your Children

Play is a significant factor in the health and development of children. Young children learn through play. Play has been found to increase cognitive development. Play allows parents an opportunity to spend quality time with their children. Whether it is a board game or a game of catch, the parents are involved and are showing interest in their children.

Pay Attention to Your Needs

Parents need to pay attention to their own health and development. Children desperately need their parents to teach and guide them. Parents needs to be healthy in order to fulfill their responsibility of effective parenting. So parents, practice making healthy choices for yourself and your family. Eat a variety of foods, and choose a diet low in fat, saturated fat, and cholesterol. Choose a diet with plenty of vegetables, fruit, and grain products, and use sugar, salt, and sodium only in moderation. Refer to the U.S. Department of Agriculture food pyramid for a guide to daily food choices.

According to recent reports from the American Heart Association, the leading causes of death for African-Americans are cardiovascular diseases and cancer. A guide for African-Americans from the National Institute of Health and the National Cancer Institute called "Spread the Word about Cancer" states that "Black Americans are diagnosed with cancer and die from it more often than any other group. But many more would survive from cancer if they make a few more changes in their diet habits."

Parents may want to return to school to take special interest courses, such as painting, a foreign language, or music; to get their GED; or to finish college. It doesn't matter what parents do. The germane point is: Parents need to devote more time to their own development. It will not only help the adults enhance their own parenting skills but it will also increase their self-esteem.

THE ROLE OF THE
AFRICAN-AMERICAN FATHER

The significance of fathers' involvement in child rearing, family activities, and school programs is usually disregarded. Very little research has been conducted on the importance of fathers' involvement in their children's education. This overlooked field of research may evolve from the perception of the male's role in the family as the primary wage earner. This perception has changed because of shifts in the labor force, which now includes a large number of mothers, including those with young children; single mothers; and mothers new to employment due to welfare-to-work legislation requiring all mothers on welfare to find a job and/or get training that will prepare them for the labor market.

According to the National Center for Education Statistics, four million babies are born each year in the United States. Of those, nearly one out of eight is born to a teenage mother; one out of four to a mother with less than a high school education; almost one out of three to a mother who lives in poverty; and one out of four to an unmarried mother.

A large number of African-American children are at risk of academic failure and failure in life if more African-American males do not become involved in their children's development. Many African-American children are exposed to factors that contribute to their educational disadvantage and failure, such as poverty, violence, crime, low self-esteem, and diminished hope and faith in society and in life. According to the Bureau of the Census, in 1996, 54.2 percent of African-American children lived with their mother only. The poverty rate for children is higher if they live with only one parent.

Recent research on the contributions fathers make to their children's development should send a strong message to all fathers to get involved and participate in their children's upbringing. Psychologists have found that when fathers are involved with their children, their social, emotional, and cognitive development skills are enhanced. The role of the father is very critical to the son. Research has found that the nurturing fathers give to their sons dramatically increases their ability to learn. Close father-son relationships have been found to increase the son's development of analytic skills. According to the U.S. Department of Justice, "Children who have an on-going positive connection to their fathers do better in school and get along better with their peers than children without such a relationship. Those children whose fathers play a positive role in their lives also tend to stay out of the juvenile justice system."

I have noticed from my experience in working with and counseling young parents—some not so young, but with limited knowledge of parenting—that a lot of African-American fathers want to participate in their children's development and be responsible fathers but many barriers prevent them from doing so. These barriers include noncustodial rights; fathers not married to the children's mother; and the most frequent barrier I encounter, the mother denying access to and participation by the father as punishment to the father because he and the mother are not together. In my counseling sessions I inform the mother about the significance of the father's participation in the child's development, and advise the mother that it is in the best interest of the child's social, emotional, and cognitive development to allow the father to participate in his child's development.

According to Stephen J. Foster, an executive with an electronics firm in San Diego, and a father of four children, writing in *Essence* magazine, "Most of us want to have a relationship with our kids. But for some dads the problem is simple: we just never learn how." There is an unfair myth that African-American fathers from low-income and high-risk backgrounds do not participate in child rearing responsibilities. In my work with young children I have seen African-American fathers from all levels of the socioeconomic ladder participate in their children's learning. They bring their children to, and pick them up from school; the fathers ask about homework; and they attend parent-teacher conferences and parenting workshops.

More African-American men must start now—before it's too late—to work with at-risk children to help them learn.

One of the primary agents of change in children's success or failure is setting goals. Goals help parents and children establish clearly defined objectives and a definite purpose, which will serve as guideposts for academic and career success.

CHAPTER 10

The Importance of Setting Goals and Academic Standards for Your Children

Parents have the most influence to effect change in children's learning and success. Parents can help their children become successes instead of failures; honor roll students instead of school dropouts. One of the primary agents of change is setting goals. Goals help parents and children establish clearly defined objectives and a definite purpose, which will serve as guideposts for academic and career success. According to Benjamin E. Mays,

> The tragedy of life doesn't lie in not reaching your goal. The tragedy lies in having no goal to reach. It isn't a calamity to die with dreams unfulfilled, but it is a calamity not to dream. It is not a disaster to be unable to capture your ideal, but it is a disaster to have no ideal to capture. It is not a disgrace not to reach the stars, but it is a disgrace to have no stars to reach for. Not failure, but low aim is a sin.

What are goals? Goals are objectives that parents and children set to work toward completing a definite purpose or mission. Goals help parents and children better plan their life's journey, aim, and destination. Goals are declarations made to self in which a specific endeavor, task, or purpose is to be accomplished. Goals are plans, outlines, or methods for achieving a desired result. Parents should develop a mission statement for their children. For example, a parents' mission statement may include the following:

> My children will begin kindergarten ready to learn with highly developed concepts in reading, writing, math, and self-help skills; they will demonstrate competencies in reading by the end of first grade; demonstrate competencies in math, algebra, and science by the end of eighth grade; take advanced courses in algebra, calculus, chemistry, and physics in high school; study foreign languages; make the honor roll in all grades; take college preparatory courses and advanced placements examinations. My children will master the academic standards at each level of development and grade, and succeed in school.

Parents should set goals at each stage or level of development. Thus,

- Infant goals
- Toddler goals
- Early childhood goals
- Middle childhood goals
- Adolescence goals

These goals should

- Be specific with a definite purpose.
- Have clearly defined completion objectives, such as short-, mid-, and long-range plans.
- Be realistic and attainable.
- Identify strengths and weaknesses of the children.
- Consider the children's needs and wants.
- Establish requirements needed to complete the goals.
- Follow a schedule for completion.

Parents and children should

- Evaluate their goals, and revise them if necessary.

- Establish a reward system for goal completion.
- Set new goals when others are mastered.

Here are some questions parents should consider regarding their children's goals.

Infant Stage Goals (0–12 months)

- What are your goals to help your infant learn?
- What are your goals to ensure that your infant is healthy and remains healthy?
- What are your goals to help your infant feel safe and secure?
- What are your goals for stimulating your infant's brain?
- What are your goals for building self-esteem in your infant?

Toddler Stage Goals (12–24 months)

- What are your goals to encourage language development in your toddler?
- What are your goals for promoting and encouraging independence?
- What are your goals for helping your child to develop beginning reading skills?
- What are your goals for helping your child develop social skills, such as family rules, self-awareness, and awareness and understanding of others?
- What are you goals to help your child learn to share?

Early Childhood Goals (2–5 years)

- What goals do you have for enhancing your child's cognitive skills?
- What are your goals for developing your child's social skills?
- What are your goals for building self-esteem?
- What are your goals for helping your child to learn history and the contributions African-Americans have made to society?

- What specific reading concepts do you expect your child to achieve, such as understanding the relationship between pictures, words, and numbers, and letter and word recognition?

Middle Childhood Goals (6–12 years)

- What are your goals to help your child become self-sufficient?
- What are your goals to help your child deal with peer pressure?
- What are your goals to enhance your child's positive self-identity?
- What are your child's goals?
- What are your specific academic goals such as reading and writing abilities?

Adolescence Goals (12–19 years)

- What are your goals for helping your child find his or her ideal self?
- What are your goals for building and enhancing self-esteem in your child?
- What are your goals for helping your child to become self-sufficient and self-determined?
- What are your child's goals?
- What specific academic goals do you have for your child such as taking advanced high school courses in math and science?

Parents can use Table 10.1, as an example, to help plan short-range goals in the core areas of reading, writing, mathematics, science, social studies, and life self-help skills. Parents may add subjects depending on the specific goals for their children. Table 10.2 can help parents plan mid- and long-range academic goals in primary school, elementary school, middle school, high school, and college or trade school. Parents may add subjects such as foreign language, psychology, music, dance, computer science, theater, or other subjects depending on the specific goals and interests of their children.

High standards, goals, and expectations help children increase their knowledge and academic performance in all subject areas. High standards, goals, and expectation motivate children to work harder. When children work harder and study more information, they learn more. Children cannot learn what they do not study. Parents as partners in their children's education should share with the children's teacher their goals, standards, and academic expectations. Parents should find out the schools' academic standards, and if they do not have standards, encourage and work with the schools to develop high standards for all children.

A Special Note about the Internet

All African-American children should learn how to use computers and the Internet, sometimes called the information superhighway. The Internet is a worldwide network of computers that connects schools, organizations, businesses, and individuals. The Internet allows users to communicate and send and receive information from friends and associates worldwide. Electronic mail (E-mail) allows users to electronically receive or mail messages to other users who have E-mail addresses. Users can send or post messages to various Internet discussion groups through electronic bulletin boards. Another part of the Internet is called the World Wide Web (www or the Web). The Web allows documents on the Internet to incorporate pictures and sound. One of the most important benefits of the Internet, especially to children, is the wide variety of available educational information. The Internet is a natural learning vehicle for children because of their innate propensity to explore, discover, create, and learn. All children are curious and have a desire to interact with their environment.

There are many sites on the Internet that can help children learn and succeed in school and in life. Children can explore fossils, temperature, rain forests, and the universe; watch space

Table 10.1. Short-range goal planning.

Subject	Pre-school	Kinder-garten	1st grade	2nd grade	3rd grade	4th grade	5th grade	6th grade	7th grade	8th grade	9th grade	10th grade	11th grade	12th grade	College or trade school
Reading															
Writing															
Math															
Science															
Social studies															
Life self-help skills															

	Table 10.2. What goals and skills do you expect your child to master in the following subjects?				
Subject	**Primary school (Grades K–2)**	**Elementary school (Grades 3–6)**	**Middle school (Grades 7–8)**	**High school (Grades 9–12)**	**College or trade school**
Reading					
Writing					
Math					
Science					
Social studies					
Life self-help skills					

explorations; research and relive historical events; go on a guided tour of the White House; study the art, history, and culture of African-Americans; find help with homework; take a college course; play games; and communicate with others worldwide using E-mail and electronic bulletin boards. If parents do not have a computer at home, many local libraries have computers and Internet access. Also, many schools allow their computers to be used by students and their families.

I have listed some of the sites and Web addresses that I recommend for African-American children and families in the appendix. This is not a complete listing, but can be useful to parents and children to quickly access some of the best educational and informational Web sites. This list can also save valuable time. Internet addresses are current as of the publication year in this book. Internet home addresses are somewhat like people, they move at times. If you cannot access the Web site listed in this book, use one of the search features on your Web browser to get the current address.

All African-American children should learn how to use computers and the internet. There are many sites on the internet that can help children learn and succeed in school and in life.

Children's Safety on the Internet

The Internet is akin to television. As noted, there are a wide array of educational and informational advantages of using the Internet; but there can be disadvantages and risks to children navigating the information superhighway.

The Internet has many sites that are inappropriate for children, including access to information and channels that have violence, racism, child pornography, obscene materials, and sexual predators.

Like television and other media, parents should

- Monitor the amount of time children spend surfing the Internet. Too much time spent in cyberspace can limit the time needed for school studies and homework completion.

- Spend time surfing the Internet with their children. This helps monitor the program content to which children are exposed. This is an excellent opportunity for parents to spend qualitative time participating in their children's learning by exploring the universe, learning about people and events in African-American history, or finding answers for homework assignments or other questions children wish to explore.
- Teach children the potential risks and hazards of using the Internet and E-mail. Teach them ways they can protect themselves, such as never giving out personal information including full names, home and school addresses, home and school telephone numbers, and passwords. Teach children that all people on the Internet are not good, and that children should never agree to meet anyone in person that they meet on-line unless the parent approves and goes with them.
- Restrict children's access to inappropriate channels and Web sites by using the Internet service provider's Parent Control or Internet Access Custom Control settings to create screen names for their children and/or to limit or block E-mail to children's accounts. American Online, one of the most popular and family-friendly service providers, has a kids' only account that is recommended for children ages 12 and under. The Kids Only account limits children's Internet access to the Kids Only channel. Children assigned to the Kids Only channel are restricted from sending instant messages, entering chat rooms, and using premium services; they are allowed to receive text-only electronic mail.

There are many companies offering parental control software, which is designed to protect children from inappropriate materials. The software provides channel tracking and monitoring devices to help parents monitor their children's Internet use when they are not being directly supervised. A list of parental control resources can be found on the SafeKids Web site at http://www.safekids.com/filters.htm.

For a monthly fee, Internet service providers, such as America Online, AT&T, GTE, CompuServe, Prodigy, and MCI provide the software users need. There are also many local companies providing Internet access services. Parents should investigate the children's safety features and parental control capacities, as well as the monthly fees, as deciding factors for selecting an Internet service provider. Remember, the best way to ensure the safety of children on the Internet is to become involved in your children's World Wide Web pursuits and to continue to monitor and supervise their Internet activities.

Recommended Resources for African-American Children

WEB SITES

Afro-America: The Black History Museum

http://www.afroam.org/history/history.html

This site contains on-line interactive exhibits on slavery, the Tuskegee Airmen, and Jackie Robinson and his challenge to be the first African-American to play baseball in the major leagues.

Afrocentric

http://eb-p5.eb.uah.edu/~nsbe/textonly/afrocent.html

This site provide links to other Web sites serving the needs of African-Americans.

Afrocentric

http://eb-p5.eb.uah.edu/org/nsbe/afrocent.html

The Black Collegian On-line offers information on college life and events on university campuses.

African-American History

http://www.msstate.edu/Archives/History/USA/
Afro-Amer/afro.html

This site provides guides and links to African-American history.

African-American Mosaic Exhibition

http://lcweb.loc.gov/exhibits/african/intro.html

This is a Library of Congress resource guide for the study of black history and culture covering nearly 500 years of the black experience in the western hemisphere.

African-American Museums and Historical Societies

http://www2.lib.udel.edu/subj/blks/internet/afammus.htm

This site is a guide to other Internet resources.

African-American Warriors

http://www.abest.com/~cklose/aawar.htm

This site is dedicated to African-Americans in the Civil War.

Amistad Links

http://www.amistad.org/

This site links users to pages about the history of the ship, the *Amistad* its revolt, and the legal challenges to win its passengers' freedom.

American Slave Narratives

http://xroads.virginia.edu/~HYPER/wpa/wpahome.html

The American Slave narrative provides an on-line anthology of slavery, and allows Web surfers to view photographs.

African-American Perspectives

http://lcweb2.loc.gov/ammem/aap/aaphome.html

The Daniel A. P. Murray Pamphlet Collection presents a perspective of African-American history and culture from the early nineteenth century through the early twentieth century. Frederick Douglass, Booker T. Washington, Ida B. Wells-Barnett, Benjamin W. Arnett, Alexander Crummel, and Emanuel Love are some of the authors represented.

UGA African-American Studies

http://www.uga.edu/~iaas/History.html

This Web site showcases African-American history.

American Library Association

http://www.ala.org/parentspage/greatsites/amazing.html

This site includes a wide variety of information for both children and adults. It offers links to over 700 other sites. The site includes KidsConnect, a question-and-answer, on-line referral service for K–12 students, and educational games. Parents can find information about award-winning books and material for children.

American Library Association

http://www.ala.org/parentspage/greatsites/parent.html

This is one of the premiere sites for parents, caregivers, teachers, and others who provide services to children. The site provides important information and resources that parents and caregivers can use to help children learn.

American Library Association : Sites for Children

http://www.ala.org/parentspage/greatsites/earth.html

This children's site presents information on animals, dinosaurs, zoos and aquariums, weather and the environment, geology and science, and astronomy and space.

http://www.ala.org/parentspage/greatsites/science.html

This children's site has educational information about general science, chemistry and physics, biology, mathematics, computers and technology, and science experiments.

Black Facts On-line

http://www.blackfacts.com/

This site provides Internet resources for black history information.

Black History Search: Education

http://www.ai.mit.edu/~isbell/Hfh/black/searchKeys.doit?
query=education

This site allows users access to interesting facts about black history. Users may search for information by month, by year, or by using a keyword search for a particular topic.

Black Talk

http://www.blacktalk.com/

Black Talk is involved in the global exchange of information and ideas.

Boston African-American NHS Home Page

http://www.cr.nps.gov/boaf/

The site includes 15 pre-Civil War structures relating to the history of Boston's nineteenth century African-American community. The sites are linked by the Black Heritage Trail, Augustus Saint-Gaudens' memorial to Robert Gould Shaw, and the African-American Massachusetts 54th Regiment.

A Deeper Shade of History: Events and Folks in Black History

http://www.ai.mit.edu/~isbell/Hfh/black/bhist.html

This is a black history database.

Stamp on Black History Home Page

http://library.advanced.org/10320/Stamps.htm

This site presents black men and women who have made significant contributions to American history.

Cool Kids Stuff

http://www.acekids.com/kidshome.html

This site provides stories and games for children and help with homework problems.

Exploratorium: ExploraNet

http://www.exploratorium.edu/

The Exploratorium is an on-line museum of science, art, and human perception with over 500 interactive, hands-on exhibits. Children can learn about memory, take a memory test, or use the science explorer to make a sun clock.

Frederick Douglass National Historic Site

http://www.nps.gov/ncro/nace/freddoug.html

This site provides an address where users can write for information about Frederick Douglass or his home at Cedar Hill.

The Franklin Institute Science Museum

http://sin.fi.edu/

Children can view on-line science and technology exhibits at this site.

The History Place Presents Abraham Lincoln

http://www.historyplace.com/lincoln/index.html

This is an excellent research source site for students. It shows the complete life of Abraham Lincoln through words, photographs, and a timeline.

The Internet Kids and Family Yellow Pages

http://www.netmom.com/ikyp/samples/hot_homework.htm

Children can find help with homework at this site.

Internet Connections/Life Skills

http://www.mcrel.org/connect/life.html

This site provides links to educational resources and information sites that help students develop life skills.

Internet Connections

http://www..mcrel.org/connect/index.html

This is a link to educational resources for children.

Internet Connections/Science

http://www..mcrel.org/connect/science.html

This site provides links to resources and educational sites that enhance the study of science.

Introducing JASON X!

http://www.jasonproject.org/expedition/jason10/index.html

Children can explore fossils, temperature, and rain forests of the earth, and discover the mysteries of past and present rainforests.

Jean Amour Polly's 50 Extraordinary Experiences

http://www.well.com/user/polly/ikyp.exp.html

This site includes suggestions for 100 great sites in 10 categories for children and parents.

K–12 Topics

http://www.mckinley.com/magellan/Re.../Education/
K-12/index.magellan.html

Users at this site find specific information about elementary, middle, and high schools. Facts such as the academic standards, administration and services, awards, and academic achievements of each school are included.

Kids' Corner

http://www.rollanet.org/kids/

This site provides links to other interesting and exciting children's sites.

Kwanzaa Information Center

http://www.melanet.com/kwanzaa/

This is an on-line source for Kwanzaa information and gifts.

Library of Congress Home Page

http://www..loc.gov/

The Library of Congress Web site provides children access to documents, photographs, movies, and recordings about America's history and to current bills under consideration in the U.S. House of Representatives and the U.S. Senate.

The Martin Luther King, Jr. Center for Nonviolent Social Change

449 Auburn Avenue, N.E.
Atlanta, GA 30312
(404) 524-1956

http://www.thekingcenter.com/

The King Center was established in 1968 by Mrs. Coretta Scott King as a living memorial dedicated to preserving the legacy of her husband, Dr. Martin Luther King, Jr., and promoting the elimination of poverty, racism, and war through research, education, and training. The Center for Nonviolent Social Change is dedicated to carrying forward the legacy and work of Dr. King through research, education, and training in the principles, philosophy, and methods of nonviolence. The King papers project includes speeches, sermons, correspondence, and personal papers. The King Library has the largest collection of materials on King and the Civil Rights Movement.

Martin Luther King, Jr. Papers Project at Stanford University

http://www-lcland.stanford.edu/group/King/

This Web site contains secondary documents written about Martin Luther King, Jr., as well as primary documents written during King's life.

Martin Luther King, Jr. Links

http://www-land.stanford.edu/group/King/Links/index.htm

This site provide links to other pages about Dr. Martin Luther King, Jr.

My Virtual Reference Desk

http://www.refdesk.com/

This is an excellent research source students can use to find facts and information, a virtual encyclopedia, and tutorial and learning guides.

My Virtual Reference Desk—My Homework Helper

http://www.refdesk.com/homework.html

At this site, students can find help with homework in reading, writing, math, English, social studies, and science for all grades through college.

NASA: Structure and Evolution of the Universe

http://universe.gsfc.nasa.gov/new/home.html

At this site, children and parents can follow NASA's efforts to discover and explore the universe by watching audio and video transmissions of various explorations.

NASA Spacelink—An Aeronautics and Space Resource for Educators

http://spacelink.nasa.gov/index.html

This is an aeronautics and space resource for educators and parents.

Parents and Children Together On-line

http://www.indiana.edu/~eric_rec/fl/ras.html

This is a project of the Family Literacy Center that publishes a magazine for parents and children on the World Wide Web. The magazine's goal is to further the cause of family literacy by bringing together parents and children through the magic of reading.

Sailor: Inventory of African-American and Cultural Resources in Maryland

http://sailor.lib.md.us/docs/af_am/af_am.html

This site provide an inventory of African-American historical and cultural resources in Maryland.

Welcome to the White House

http://www.whitehouse.gov/WH/Welcome.html

This site provides a virtual tour of the White House for parents and children.

The White House for Kids

http://www.whitehouse.gov/WH/kids/html/home.html

Children can go on an on-line guided tour of the White House, which is organized into six sections: (1) Where is the White House; (2) The History of the White House; (3) Our President; (4) Children in the White House; (5) Pets in the White House; and (6) Write to the President.

LIBRARY AND RESEARCH RESOURCES

Africana Collection

http://www.uflib.ufledu/hss/africana/

The University of Florida's George A. Smathers Libraries African

Collection is a remarkable source to find other African resources and references.

Africana at the University of Illinois Library

http://wsi.sco.uiuc.edu/CAS/Library/lib.html

The University of Illinois Library has an extensive African collection. It is the third largest library in the country, and is a good source for research on the study of Africa.

Africana Collection

http://www.library.nwu.edu/africana/

Students will find the Northwestern University Library African collection to be the supreme collection for the research and study of Africa.

Africa: Library and Information Resources

http://www.-sul.stanford.edu/depts/ssrg/africa/africa.html

This site collects infinite amounts of materials on African history and government.

African-American Studies

http://www.geocities.com/CollegePark/Quad/9594/

This Web site has a variety of things surfers can do. They can take a quiz about African-American issues, learn about interesting African-American books to read, and link with related Web sites.

African and African-American Collections at UC Berkeley

http://www.lib.berkeley.edu/Collections/Africana/

These collections at the University of California–Berkeley are excellent research sources in African and African-American studies. The collections are extensive.

African-American Museums and Historical Societies

http://www2.libudel.edu/subj/blks/internet/afammus.htm

This is a guide to Internet resources of interest to African-Americans.

African Language and Literature Collection

http://www.indiana.edu/~libresd/afrig/

This is a wonderful collection of African language and literature at Indiana University Libraries in Bloomington.

African Library Resources at the University of Pennsylvania

http://www.sas.upenn.edu/African_Studies/Bibliography/PNN_Afrik.html

This Web site is in progress but has good potential for research once the University of Pennsylvania goes on-line with its library research on Africa.

African Studies Internet Resources

http://www.columbia.ecu/cu/libraries/indiv/area/Africa/

Columbia University's African Studies Internet resources is one of the supreme on-line sources for African studies.

African Studies Library Home Page

http://software2.bu.edu/LIBRARY/ASL/home.html

Boston's University's African Studies Library has a wonderful source of current information about Africa.

The African World Community Network

http://www.he.net/~awe/

This site provides links to other Web sites of interest to African-Americans.

The *Amistad* Research Center

http://www.arc.tulane.edu/

The mission of this premier Web site is the preservation of African-American history and culture.

Black Film Center/Archive Home Page

http://www.indiana.edu/~bfca/index.html

This is a repository of films and related materials by and about African-Americans.

Black Studies

http://www.lib.ohio-state.edu/OSU_profile/bslweb/

The Ohio State University Libraries Black Studies Web site is a good reference and resource for the cultures of Africa and African-Americans.

CAAS–UCLA

http://www.sscnet.ucla.edu/caas/

The UCLA Center for African-American Studies provides programs and research with an emphasis on African-American studies.

CSADP

http://diaspora.sscnet.ucla.edu/

The CSADP Web site is UCLA's African Diaspora Cultural Studies project with research information on post-colonial, transnational migratory, and post-slavery communities.

The Center for Research Libraries

http://wwwcrl.uchicago.edu/info/camp.htm

This site is a Cooperative Africana Microform Project involved in promoting and preserving materials from Sub-Saharan Africa.

Dartmouth Library Collection Development Policy

http://www.dartmouth.edu/~cmdc/aaas.html

The African and African-American Studies Web site at Dartmouth College Library is an important source for African, Caribbean, and African-American studies.

The John Henrik Clarke Africana Library

http://www.library.cornell.edu/africana/

Cornell University's John Henrik Clarke African Library has an impressive collection on Africa's history and culture.

Howard University

http://www.howard.edu/hu-homepages/Welcome.htm

The Ralph J. Bunch International Affairs Center is a source for students researching international and global issues.

Michigan State University Library and Africana Collections

http://www.isp.msu.edu/AfricanStudies/africana.htm

The African Studies Center has an enormous Africana collection along with related resources and materials.

Museums and Organizations

http://www.si.edu/organiza/start.htm

This Web site provides an overview from the Smithsonian Institute of museums, organizations, events, activities, tours, and resources.

UCLA Library Sub-Saharan Africa

http://www.library.ucla.edu/libraries/url/colls/ssafrica/index.htm

The UCLA Library Collections and Internet Resources in African Studies provide valuable tools to students who are researching on-line Sub-Saharan Africa and the islands of the Indian and Atlantic Oceans.

University of Iowa: Center for Electronic Resources in African Studies

http://staffweb.lib.uiowa.edu/tlyles/african/

This is a "library in the sky" offering students an abundance of resources in African studies.

W. E. B. Du Bois Institute for Afro-American Research

http://web-dubois.fas.harvard.edu/

The W. E. B. Du Bois Institute has been one of the leaders in the research and study of African history and culture.

MUSEUMS

African and African-American Resources at the Smithsonian

Smithsonian Institute
MRC, 010
Washington, DC 20560
(202) 357-2700
E-mail: viarc.info@ic.si.edu.

http://www.si.edu/resource/tours/afafam/start.htm

There is a wide array of African-American resources at the Smithsonian Institute including the following: the Anacostia Museum, which exhibits the art, history, culture, and contributions of African-Americans; the Archives of American Art, which includes more than 80 African-American painters, sculptors, and print makers from the late nineteenth century to the present; the Center for African-American History; the National Museum of African Art; and more. This Web site is rich in information and resources on African-Americans. To receive copies of the brochure "African and African-American Resources at the Smithsonian," write or E-mail the Smithsonian Institute at address shown.

African-American Museum in Cleveland

1765 Crawford Rd.
Cleveland, OH 44106
(216) 791-1700

http://www.ben.net/aamuseum/index.htm

This site provides Web surfers with a virtual tour of African-American history.

African-American Museum in Philadelphia

701 Arch St.
Philadelphia, PA 19106
(215) 574-0380

http://libertynet.org./iha/tour/ afrc.html

This museum takes users on an extraordinary virtual tour of the history of Philadelphia's African-American community. Viewers can visit museums, famous houses, or the Liberty Bell. The Liberty Bell is the bell that made history when it was used to assemble citizens to hear the first public reading of the Declaration of Independence. The Liberty Bell is so famous it has its own Web site. The Liberty Bell Home Page is http://www.libertynet.org/iha/libertybell.

African Heritage Cultural Center

Detroit Public School
21511 W. McNichols Rd.
Detroit, MI 48219
Fax: (313) 494-7452

http://dpsnet.detpub.k12.mi.us./heritage/

This museum and its Web site provide information on the origin of man and the discovery of the earliest hominid fossil remains. African-like pyramid buildings; great West African empires; Mekeda, known as the queen of Sheba; and early African civilizations are also featured.

Birmingham Civil Rights Institute

520 Sixteenth St. North
Birmingham, AL 35203
(205) 328-9696

http://www.bham.net/bcri/index.html

The Birmingham Civil Rights Institute captures the individuals who dared to confront racism and fought discrimination and bigotry. Special features include a burned-out bus, chronicles of the Montgomery Bus Boycott and other events, and artifacts such as the actual door from the jail cell where Dr. Martin Luther King, Jr. wrote his letter from a Birmingham jail.

California African-American Museum

600 State Dr.
Exposition Park
Los Angeles, CA 90037
(213) 744-7432

http://www.caam.ca.gov/

The museum's site provides excellent Web links to California government Web sites, the California State Museum, and to some other African-American Web sites.

Chattanooga African-American Museum

200 E. Martin Luther King Blvd.
Chattanooga, TN 37403
(423) 266-8658

http://webusers.anet-stl.com/~afields/caam/caam.html

On-line users can explore the history of African-Americans in Chattanooga, and learn about successful African-American people established in the 1800s, including African-American factory owners, doctors, and lawyers. Users are able to experience the life of the early African-American settlement and view African-American towns.

DuSable Museum of African-American History

740 E. 56th Pl.
Chicago, IL 60637
(773) 947-0600

http://www.dusable.org/index.shtml

This is Chicago's premier African-American museum, which preserves and showcases the history of African-Americans. Visitors will find enchanting exhibits, a cinema series, children's theater, and special events.

The Museum of African-American History

315 E. Warren Ave.
Detroit, MI 48201
(313) 494-5800

http://www.detroitnews.com/maah

This museum is dedicated to the preservation and presentation of African-American history and culture.

Museum of African-American Life and Culture

3536 Grand Ave.
Dallas, TX
(214) 565-9026

http://www.expedia.msn.com/wg/places/Un...tates/Dallas-FortWorth/A10500018.htm

This museum has an immense collection of African-American folk art. Students can also find information relating to African-American women in their African-American Worker's Archives.

Museum of Afro American History Boston

138 Mountfort St.
Brookline, MA 02146
(617) 739-1200

http://www.afroammuseum.org/index.htm

This remarkable Web site take users on a virtual walking tour that explores the captivating history of Boston's African-Americans who lived during the nineteenth century.

National Afro-American Museum and Cultural Center

1350 Brush Row Rd.
P.O. Box 578
Wilberforce, OH 45384
Museum: (937) 376-4944
Black History: (800) 255-4478

http://www.ohiohistory.org/places/afroam

This museum and cultural center's mission is to foster African-American history and culture by collecting, preserving, and interpreting materials and evidence of the black experience.

National Civil Rights Museum

450 Mulberry St.
Memphis, TN 38103
(901) 521-9699

http://www.mecca.org/~crights/

The National Civil Rights Museum is located at the Lorraine Motel in Memphis, Tennessee where Dr. Martin Luther King was assassinated. The goal of the museum is to instill in others the importance of the Civil Rights Movement and the events and people involved.

Oakes African-American Museum

Intersection of Hwy 49W & Hwy 3
117 Haley Barbour Pkwy.
Yazoo City, MS 39194
(601) 746-1815 or (800) 381-0662

http://www.yazoo.org/museum.html

This Web site documents the history and culture of African-

Americans in this unique Mississippi county. Visitors learn how many African-Americans succeeded in spite of great odds.

Tubman African-American Museum

340 Walnut St.
Macon, GA 31201
(912) 743-8544

http://www.mid-georgia.com/tubman/

This is Georgia's largest African-American museum. Visitors can explore and learn about African-American cultural heritage and view exhibits on African-American leaders and artists.

OTHER ORGANIZATIONS

American Academy of Pediatrics

141 Northwest Point Blvd.
Elk Grove Village, IL 60007-1098
(847) 228-5005
Fax: (847) 228-5097

http://www.aap.org/

The AAP provide parents with a variety of information on infant care and children's health and development.

Association for the Study of Afro-American Life and History

1407 14th St., NW
Washington, DC 20005
(202) 667-2822
Fax: (202) 387-9802

http://www.artnoir.com/asalh/

This association supports the study of Afro-American history through various institutions and by sponsoring workshops and seminars. It is the co-sponsor of the National History Day program, and presents the Carter G. Woodson Awards to high school students for various projects relating to Afro-American history.

ASPIRA Association, Inc.

1444 I St., NW, 8th Floor
Washington, DC 20005
(202) 835-3600

http://incacorp.com/aspira

This is a national organization empowering to serve Puerto Rican and Latin children through education and leadership development programs. ASPIRA works to unite teachers and parents in a partnership to help children succeed.

Chicago Council on Black Studies

http://sol.plp.uic.edu/equinox.html

E-mail: pricevo@uic.edu
This is a coalition of local academics and administrators from university black studies departments and programs, other academic departments and programs, and community-based programs and institutions concerned with teaching the African-American experience.

Children's Defense Fund

25 E St., NW
Washington, DC 20001
(202) 628-8787

http://www.childrensdefense.org/

The Children Defense Fund lobbies for children's rights, and educates the nation about the needs of children.

The Children's Partnership

1351 3RD Street promenade, Suite 206
Santa Monica, CA 90401
(310) 260-1220

http://www.childrenspartnership.org/

This organization lobbies the needs of children to policymakers and the private sector; conducts research; and publishes reports and multimedia materials relating to children.

The Family Education Network

20 Park Plaza, Suite 1215
Boston, MA 02116
(617) 542-6500, ext. 127

http://familyeducation.com/vcenter.asp

This organization provides information and resources to help families and their children learn. Information includes homework help, after-school activities, and news and education policy.

NAACP

1025 Vermont Ave., NW, Suite 1120
Washington, DC 20005
(202) 638-2269

http://www.naacp.org/

The National Association for the Advancement of Colored People is the oldest civil rights organization in the United States. The principal objective of the NAACP is to ensure the political, educational, social, and economic equality of minority group citizens in the United States.

National Black Child Development Institute

1023 15th St., NW, Suite 600
Washington, DC 20005
(202) 387-1281

http://www.nbcdi.org/

NBCDI works to improve and protect the quality of life of
African-American children and their families.

National Coalition for Parent Involvement
in Education

1201 16th St. NW, Box 39
Washington, DC 20036
(202) 822-8405

http://www.ncpie.org/

NCPIE develops family-school partnerships, and advocates for
parent/family participation in their children's education.

National PTA

Patricia Yoxall, Director of Public Relations
330 N. Wabash Ave, Suite 2100
Chicago, IL 60611
(312) 670-6782
E-mail: info@pta.org

http://www.pta.org/index.stm

The National PTA is the oldest and largest volunteer association
in the United States, working exclusively on behalf of children
and youth.

National Urban League

120 Wall St.
New York, NY 10005
(212) 558-5300
E-mail: infor@nul.org

http://www.nul.org

The National Urban League works to assist African-Americans in the achievement of social and economic equality.

ACTIVITY GUIDE

MISSION STATEMENT

I. Develop a mission statement for your children.

LOW SELF-ESTEEM

II. A child with low self-esteem exhibits the following negative characteristics.

1.

2.

3.

4.

5.

6.

7.

8.

9.

10.

HIGH SELF-ESTEEM

III. A child with high self-esteem exhibits the following positive characteristics.

1.

2.

3.

4.

5.

6.

7.

8.

9.

10.

THE NEEDS OF CHILDREN

IV. Name ten needs of children.

    1.

    2.

    3.

    4.

    5.

    6.

    7.

    8.

    9.

    10.

LEARNING BEGINS AT HOME

V. Name five things you will do in the home to help your children learn.

1.

2.

3.

4.

5.

PARENTS CAN HELP THEIR CHILDREN SUCCEED IN SCHOOL

VI. Name five things you will do in your children's school to help them succeed.

1.

2.

3.

4.

5.

GUIDEPOSTS FOR SUCCESS
(Fill in the blank)

VII. Parents take 60 minutes each day to help your children build the skills necessary for success.

    1. **TAKE 10** minutes to _____ to your children.

    2. **TAKE 10** minutes to _____ to your children.

    3. **TAKE 10** minutes to _____ to your children.

    4. **TAKE 10** minutes to _____ to your children.

    5. **TAKE 10** minutes to _____ to your children.

    6. **TAKE 10** minutes to _____ to your children.

INFANT STAGE GOALS

VIII. What are your children's infant stage goals?

1.

2.

3.

4.

5.

6.

7.

8.

9.

10.

TODDLER STAGE GOALS

IX. What are your children's toddler stage goals?

1.

2.

3.

4.

5.

6.

7.

8.

9.

10.

EARLY CHILDHOOD GOALS

X. What are your children's early childhood goals?

1.

2.

3.

4.

5.

6.

7.

8.

9.

10.

MIDDLE CHILDHOOD GOALS

XI. What are your children's middle childhood goals?

1.

2.

3.

4.

5.

6.

7.

8.

9.

10.

ADOLESCENCE GOALS

XII. What are your children's adolescence goals?

1.

2.

3.

4.

5.

6.

7.

8.

9.

10.

INDEX

INFORMATION AND ORDER FORM

FOR INFORMATION

For more information about books, tapes, workshops, lectures, seminars, or educational products by Will Horton, use the coupon below. Send it to:

Will Horton
PO Box 17787
Chicago, IL 60617
Telephone: 773-721-7500
1-800-649-7670
Fax: 773-721-7560
E-mail: will.horton@gte.net

Name (Please print)

Address

City   State   Zip

Telephone (business)   Telephone (home)

E-mail (business)   E-mail (home)

TO ORDER

Please send me _____ copies of *Success Guideposts for African-American Children,* price $24.95 per book.

Please send me _____ copies of *The ABC's of Self-Esteem,* price $9.95 per book.

Please send me _____ copies of Positive Mind Concepts™ for children (2 audio tapes), price $20.00 per set.

Please send me _____ copies of Positive Mind Concepts™ for adults (1 audio tape), price $10.00 per tape.

Tax: Illinois residents, please add 8.75% sales tax.

Shipping charges: $3.95 for the first book or audio tape package. Add $1.00 for each additional book or tape.

Payment: ☐ Check enclosed   ☐ Credit card   ☐ Visa
☐ Master Card   ☐ Discover   ☐ American Express

Credit card number _____ Expiration date _____

_____
Name on card

_____
Address

_____
City   State   Zip

ABOUT THE AUTHOR

Will Horton is an educator and educational consultant with 20 years of educational experience from early childhood to the college level. He is president of W. Whorton & Company, an educational publishing and consulting company; president of an early childhood development center; and a former college professor and administrator. He provides workshops, seminars, and specialized training programs in a variety of topics for parents, schools, government institutions, and businesses. He is also the author of *The ABCs of Self-Esteem*.